THE MAKING OF
REDBLOOD
HOTSUGAR
CHILISEX
PEPPERSMAGIK

THE MAKING OF
REDBLOOD HOTSUGAR CHILISEX PEPPERSMAGIK

JOEL McIVER

The publisher wishes to thank the Book Division at Lasgo Chrysalis London for their ongoing support in developing this series.

Published by Unanimous Ltd.
Unanimous Ltd. is an imprint of MQ Publications Ltd.
12 The Ivories, 6–8 Northampton Street, London, N1 2HY

Printed and bound in France

ISBN: 1 90331 879 3

1 2 3 4 5 6 7 8 9

Picture credits:
Cover: © Ross Halfin/Idols.
Picture section: page 113 © Ebet Roberts/Redferns; pages 114–115 © 2005 Dave Lepori, www.leporiphoto.com; page 116 © Ebet Roberts/Redferns; page 117 Paul Bergen/Redferns; page 118 (both) © Ian Dickson/Redferns; page 119 (top) © London Features International; page 119 (bottom) © Albert Ortega/Redferns; page 120 © Webphoto/Vinmag Archive Ltd.

contents

Acknowledgments

"The Righteous And The Wicked": Carlos Anaia, Adrian Ashton, Daryl Easlea, Darren Edwards, Mike Evans, Ian Glasper, Steve Harvey, Jamie Hibbard, Chris Ingham, Andy Jones, Daniel Lane, Stephen Lawson, Sian Llewellyn, Joe Matera, Martin Popoff, Scott Rowley, Paul Stenning, Carl Swann, Tommy Udo, Sarah Watson, Henry Yates, the staff of *Record Collector*, *Metal Hammer*, *Total Guitar*, *Future Music*, *Total Film*, *Bass Guitar*, *Acoustic* and *Classic Rock* magazines.

"They're Red Hot": Robin and Abi, Dad, John and Jen, the Parr, Houston-Miller, Everitt-Bossmann and Tominey families, Vinay and Ren, Dave and Dawn, Woody and Glynis, Helen and Tony, Simone, Quinn and Amy Harrington, Christof Leim, Frank Livadaros, the Barnes, Ellis, Johnston, Legerton and Maynard dynasties.

Dedication

This book is dedicated to my lovely girls, Emma and Alice.

Blood stains cannot be removed by more blood
(*Buddha*)

The little ant tastes joyously the sweetness of honey and **sugar**
(*Sivananda*)

Of all **sexual** aberrations, chastity is the strangest
(*Anatole France*)

The power of thought, the **magic** of the mind!
(*Byron*)

introduction

Blood Sugar Sex Magik is an album to celebrate. Looking back at California—the environment which spawned it—from a decade's distance, the early 1990s were a confusion of images and sounds: the LA riots, a troubled US economy, Gulf War I, the rise (and fall) of Generation X... the outstanding memories we retain of those days are usually of the very good, or the very bad, cultural phenomena that emerged from it all.

One of the former is the Red Hot Chili Peppers' fifth album, which is an explosion of sound, texture and emotion. Surrounded by the uncertainties and the high emotions of the new alternative-rock and grunge scenes and thrown into contrast by the death of the surprisingly durable hair-metal scene (an LA creation if ever there was one), records such as this needed to be powerful, stripped-down, and honest if they were to make an impact. Alongside key records of the era by Nirvana and Metallica, *Blood Sugar...* was all that and more, a celebration of funk, punk, and raw sexuality that has not dated an iota since its release. With two huge single hits—"Under The Bridge" and "Give It Away"—the album was that perfect thing in rock terms: a serious record made by decidedly non-serious musicians, four tattooed on-stage acrobats who emitted feral pheromones, gurned like schoolboys into every camera, but were consummate musicians who redefined the intertwined roles of pop, metal, and funk in the last years of the century.

The reason for *Blood Sugar Sex Magik*'s inclusion in this series of books is that the record possesses incredible depth and vision, as well as an hour's worth of scintillating music. At first hearing "just" another fully-evolved Chili Pepper-style implosion of sexual fury and good-time technicolor, the album reveals much more serious subject matter when the listener delves a little deeper beneath its multi-textured surface: singer Anthony Kiedis (an icon for our times) addresses the issues of racism, drug abuse, the environment, and bereavement with enormous courage and sensitivity. But zoom back out again and you're left with a fantastic array of music, all of it organic and all of it real. Very real.

But *Blood Sugar Sex Magik* was a prodigy, and like all prodigies its genesis was a difficult and painful one. For 20 hours a day, every day for five weeks, the Red Hot Chili Peppers threw themselves into making the album that remains—until 2005, at least—their undisputed masterpiece. Its creation wasn't easy, and its impact was hard to describe in words. But we'll try, anyway. Read on, and hold tight—it's a bumpy ride...

the context

Why the Red Hot Chili Peppers needed to make Blood Sugar Sex Magik—and why we needed them to make it

In 1991, The Red Hot Chili Peppers were at a crossroads.

Their history up until this point has been well documented. The two founder members, singer Anthony Kiedis and bassist Michael "Flea" Balzary, had been weaned on cool jazz and fiery punk and raised in the superficially sunny environment of 1970s California. The pair had endured childhood traumas, teenage fragility, drug use and abuse and, most shockingly, the death of a close friend and band member, guitarist Hillel Slovak. The Chilis had also lost their drummer, Jack Irons, who felt unable to continue with the band in the wake of his friend Slovak's death. At one point as the 1980s came to an end, Kiedis and Flea had considered calling time on the Chilis.

But their fortunes had changed. The singer and bass player had recruited two new musicians, guitarist John Frusciante and drummer Chad Smith, and against all the odds recorded their most successful album of their career to date. *Mother's Milk* was released in August 1989 and scored immediate album-chart success thanks to deft, funky tunes such as their cover of Stevie Wonder's "Higher Ground", Flea's slap-bass-driven "Nobody Weird Like Me", and an anti-drugs anthem inspired by the death of Slovak entitled "Knock Me Down".

After 1990 had been spent touring *Mother's Milk* and then taking a well-earned break, the future looked simultaneously bright and unstable for the new line-up. Would the last album be a mere fluke? A blip on the radar? Could they match its critical and commercial popularity with their next record? And would the new band, strengthened by touring, take the next step up?

If only the answers to these questions were easy to find. With the benefit of hindsight, of course, we know what glories lay ahead of the Chilis, and what terrors. But in 1991—14 years before the publication of this book—no one could have predicted where the band would turn next, what the impact of their decisions would be, and how radically the face of rock music would be changed as the result of those decisions.

As several excellent (and less than excellent) biographies of the Red Hot Chili Peppers exist, I have avoided too many discussions of the family lives, relatives, childhood experiences, and showbiz movements of the men concerned. What I have done in this book is to focus on one, glorious, freakish album which its creators will probably never surpass, as well as how events led up to its creation, its seismic local and general effects, and what it was that made it so special.

If you're surprised that I haven't written at great length about drug deaths, teddy-bear-festooned trousers, and socks on cocks, then you've missed the point...

"We work hard," wrote Flea in the liner notes of 2004's *Greatest Hits* album, a world away conceptually from the club-level act his band was 13 years earlier. His claim was no more than the truth, and its casual understatement becomes clear when you consider the Chilis' past until this point.

Much has been written about the punkish, raw roots of the band. And with good reason: they started life as a brattish, sex- and groove-obsessed outfit more concerned with the speed and dexterity of their playing and the eye-opening visuals of their shows than with the music they made. Consider the Chilis' earliest music, made in the early 1980s as the second wave of US punk reached fever pitch. Initially they had attempted to make music in the style of progressive rock in a band called Anthem, but soon ventured into harsher and more expressive territory, the latter inspired after the hip-hop movement had taken hold.

Once the three Fairfax High School students—Kiedis, Flea, and Slovak—had honed a hard-won punk style after Slovak had taught Flea the rudiments of the bass guitar, they embarked on a near-vertical learning curve. Flea learned fast, having had some musical training thanks to his family's interest in jazz. At 12, his mother took him to a concert by one of his heroes, bebop trumpeter Dizzy Gillespie. "I snuck backstage, and there's Dizzy, holding his trumpet, talking to someone," Flea remembered later. "I run up to him... and I can't even talk. I'm in awe. And he just puts his arm around me and hugs me real tight, so my head's kind of in his armpit. He smiles and just holds me there for, like, five minutes while he talks. I'm just frozen in joy—oh my God, oh my God, oh my God."

As for Kiedis, his catalyst came when he saw the pioneering rap troupe Grandmaster Flash and the Furious Five. As he later explained, "It was mind-blowing... I subconsciously vowed I would somehow create that type of energy to entertain others. I didn't have a clue how to write a song or sing, but I thought I could probably figure out how to tell a story in rhythm." The singer, a sensitive near-intellectual whose life had been buffeted constantly by the whirlwind activities of his father, the actor Blackie Dammett, was hesitantly beginning to adapt his poetry to music, encouraged by the other two musicians.

Flea's progress on the bass was rapid: he had studied the trumpet as a teenager and applied some of this awareness to his new instrument, encouraged by the cool jazz he had been absorbing since childhood and a rampant leaning towards funk. Slovak, a keen guitarist, redoubled his efforts to improve in order to keep up with Flea. Finally, a new drummer from outside the Fairfax circle, Jack Irons, was recruited for the crucially needed percussive attack that would give Flea a battleground and make them a real band. Kiedis had become a rapper-in-waiting after hearing Grandmaster Flash and the Furious Five, saying, "[they] gave me the notion that I could do something musically without being Marvin Gaye." He later told *Playboy*, "Hearing Grandmaster Flash and the Furious Five and their song 'The Message', I realized that rhyming and developing a character were another way to do it. That rap song permeated the pop consciousness of America. And I thought it was cool. You could write poetry and create stories with colors and ambience with music, and you didn't have to be a master of melody. That's when I thought I could do something of a musical nature without the training. It became a matter of whether the voice was interesting."

"Anthony and I were street kids, basically... I had a very violent upbringing," Flea later recalled of his childhood. "[My stepfather] had shoot-outs with the cops. I slept in the backyard because I was scared. In a way, it gave me freedom. By the time I was 12 or 13, I was out until three or four in the morning, carousing, on drugs." The band, it emerged, would give both men a framework in which to develop. But there was a long way to go before real progress could be made. Although their early punk obsessions—acts from LA, California, and elsewhere such as The Germs, Black Flag, Fear, and Minutemen—were complemented rapidly by a melange of influences such as Parliament-Funkadelic, Sly & The Family Stone, Miles Davis, and others, the Chilis' initial focus was a) getting seen and b) getting laid. Performing shows as Tony Flow & The Miraculously Majestic Masters Of Mayhem—a P-Funk-derived title if there ever was one—the foursome began playing shows at strip joints on the Sunset Strip, leading to the first appearances of the football socks attached to nether regions which their later drummer, Chad Smith, acidly (and accurately) referred to a few years down the line as one of the principal reasons for which people remembered his band.

By 1983 the band had adopted the slightly less cumbersome name of The Red Hot Chili Peppers and began to forge a reputation for their skewed, unpredictable live shows. After attracting management, the band secured a quick record deal with EMI and laid plans for a debut album. Young, dumb, and full of funk, the Chilis were ready to take on the world—but just as a recording schedule was due to be finalized, Flea and Kiedis's world was turned upside down by Slovak and Irons, who informed them that they would be leaving the band to work on another project called What Is

This. Rocked but determined, the bassist and singer recruited another guitarist, Jack Sherman, and a drummer, Cliff Martinez, and entered the studio anyway.

The result was 1984's *The Red Hot Chili Peppers*, a now badly dated album, although it seemed full of fire and promise on its appearance. However, it soon became apparent that the new line-up was incapable as yet of committing to tape the funky brew which they were so able to reproduce for audiences on the live stage. While the record was a competent enough set of songs for such a young band (both Flea and Kiedis were a mere 21), it didn't grab the listener particularly hard. The opening track, "True Men Don't Kill Coyotes", with its psychedelic opening declaration of "I'm gonna ride a sabretooth horse through the Hollywood Hills" promised much, but other songs such as "Buckle Down", "Green Heaven", and "Out In LA" were light fun rather than heavy funk. However, a certain college-student fanbase began to develop on the West Coast and, as punk gave way to new wave and the imported New Romantic movement from the UK gained a foothold in the more open-minded areas of California, it seemed that the Chilis' blend of grooved-up rock might be taken more seriously in future.

In 1985 Slovak and Irons returned to the fold, What Is This having folded after a single self-titled album which had been given an even more lukewarm reception than that of the Chilis. Rehearsals resumed in earnest and the four musicians—now gaining in dexterity, if not in musical economy—re-established their old bond. This time the musical results were more solid, with none other than the legendary Parliament-Funkadelic frontman George Clinton enlisted for production duties. With the help of the dreadlocked veteran, the Chilis recorded a set of more durable tunes, including the soon-to-be set favorites "Blackeyed Blonde", "Catholic School Girls Rule", "Thirty Dirty Birds", and "Yertle The Turtle". The album—nonsensically but somehow fittingly titled *Freaky Styley*—was a step forward from its predecessor, even if rave reviews were non-existent outside the locality and no sales barriers were broken.

By the middle of the decade—which was in pop music terms, at least, and from some distance, a confused barrage of often diametrically opposed musical styles looking for a foothold—the Chilis seemed to be treading water. As the 1980s passed, Kiedis would go on record about his unease at the rise of bands such as Faith No More, who both press and public perceived as being rivals and even predecessors to his band in terms of the music they played. In true journalistic fashion, writers in both America and Europe were talking with great excitement about the "funk-metal" movement, a term which seemed apt at the time but that now appears somewhat naïve. Rock bands who favored a riff-based approach, but who anchored this with a bassist who employed the slap-and-pop style pioneered in the 1970s by legendary players such as Larry Graham and Bootsy Collins, fell under the funk-metal mantle all too easily. Like all genre labels, the tag served its purpose but rapidly became too constricting to be truly useful, largely because the two best bands it clung to—the Chilis and the aforementioned FNM—wandered far enough to throw it off.

But all this lay ahead. For now, the Chilis labored alongside soon-to-be-forgottens such as Mindfunk and The Dan Reed Network on the funk-metal scene, attracting frat-boy jock crowds and amusing a percentage of the skate-punk and thrash metal audiences at the same time. 1987 saw the release of a third album, *The Uplift Mofo Party Plan*, which raised the stakes a little—yet, frustratingly, not enough. Songs like the aggressive "Fight Like A Brave"—with its shouted chorus a look-back at the old days of punk—"Special Secret Song Inside", and the Chilis' iron-hard cover of Bob Dylan's "Subterranean Homesick Blues" were good enough to secure festival and club slots, but not really sufficient to build an international following. However, a US chart position was secured by the album for the first time in the band's history: clearly something was afoot at last and the Chilis found themselves looking to the future with enthusiasm again.

The *Party Plan* album also gained the band a reputation for the open sexuality of their songs, with one song in particular, "Party On Your Pussy", leading to an unwanted reputation for frat-party boasting. As Flea recalled in later years, "We've felt trapped, we've felt cheated. When *The Uplift Mofo Party Plan* came out, I thought artistically that was a cool record. And it was getting no play at all. 'Here's the nutty, zany guys, they're at it again; they want to Party On Your Pussy'. Which was one song on one album." This element of the band's sense of humor would expand to almost philosophical levels in later years, with Kiedis in particular (the Chili Pepper most interested in sexual exploration, by his own admission—he once described himself as an "obvious ladykiller"—and the group's only serious sex symbol) elevating the subject to intellectual heights.

On the subject of sex, Kiedis told *Playboy*, "We all have our perverted side. We all have our sexual mishaps and misadventures. We all have our weaknesses and strengths, stuff that we're ashamed of and stuff that we're proud of. It's to shine a light on it. It is not to say, 'oooh, look, I got a blowjob from your sister' [a reference to a brief dalliance with Flea's sister]. Who cares? We all do this stuff, and we don't have to be so taboo about everything. And it's OK to say, 'yeah, we're all human beings and we have these natures that we keep in the closet, but I'm not going to hide behind it.'"

Perhaps the *Uplift Mofo* production team should have taken in a few Chilis shows before moving into the studio. After all, the Chilis' live act was a facet of the band's existence which could not be ignored, with Flea describing it as follows: "Skateboarding and surfing are very akin to our music. It's all about moving forward, riding the beat and grooving and thrashing and cruising. Also, skateboards have round wheels and we have round testicles. It's the phallic thing, boards and guitars. When we become big rock stars, we're gonna have a penis-shaped jet." And although they lived in California, the usual LA clichés didn't apply, he warned: "That southern California groovy, mellow hippie thing is a silly stereotype. You can find anything you want in Hollywood, all of life is there, and the high-voltage electricity that's in the Hollywood air is the feeling we choose to perpetuate... If we started worrying about what people thought of us, we'd be lost. The main thing is to make music that makes us happy, that makes our penises hard, because we're the ones that have to live with it, go out and play it every night."

"Seeing us live made a lot of difference to the production of the album," explained Flea of the new album, "as it's such a large part of what we're about. *Freaky Styley* was a great album, the tracks are great, but physically it sounds real small now. The guitar isn't live and in-your-face enough. Neither George nor the band were there at the mixdown. We left that in the hands of the mixing engineer, and he sorta lost his erection after we left, and couldn't get it up for the mix... We weren't interested in their CVs, just in whether they understood us, and [Material member] Michael Beinhorn was about the only one who did. We also seemed to get off on the same music, the same rhythms, Jimi Hendrix, Fela Kuti, Stevie Wonder, Sly & The Family Stone... A lot of producers asked us what we wanted to make—a rock record, a funk record and so on. Michael understood that we weren't trying for a defined commerciality, we just wanted to be ourselves as hard as possible. We liked good music, soulful music, and could get as much out of Billie Holiday or AC/DC as Art Blakey. We both felt that categories are bullshit, that music should be personal expression."

As interest in the band grew, record company pressure for product increased and the band recorded and released a five-track EP in 1988 entitled *The Abbey Road EP.* More notable for its album sleeve than for its contents (the quartet were depicted crossing the famous London street clad only in genital-covering sports socks, hats, and footwear, in a parody of the original Beatles LP shot), the EP kept the Chilis' name in the rock world's bloodstream, with their version of Jimi Hendrix's "Fire" a genuine standout in their canon. Nowadays, that sleeve seems incongruous: the Chilis are now so elevated above such comic, pseudo-sexual antics that their decision to step out onto that London road mostly naked seems to have come from another band entirely.

In fact, it was at this point that the Chilis' sense of humor was almost quenched forever. On June 25, 1988 Slovak overdosed on heroin and died. Irons left the band, unable to continue in the wake of his friend's death. Kiedis, struggling with his own heroin addiction, was left with Flea: both men were stricken to the core with grief and cast around for a solution to their predicament. None was forthcoming but, rather than abandon the group which they had spent so much time building, the duo decided to continue their work. But the immense sadness which had penetrated them clung bitterly to them: it would be a long time before they could address it. Flea recalled, "Hillel's death was just devastating. I was so shocked when it happened, I just fell on the floor, gasping for air. As we started getting older, and drugs became more and more prevalent, Hillel started having a deep sadness to him. I didn't really know how to deal with that sadness, and I don't think he knew how to deal with it."

A brief liaison with former Parliament guitarist Blackbird McKnight and former Dead Kennedys drummer D.H. Peligro followed, but for reasons which have never been adequately explained, the new group didn't gel and sessions were abandoned soon after they started. Perhaps the synthesis of classic funk and classic punk was too obvious a way forward for the band, even one as steeped in the two musical genres as the Red Hot Chili Peppers: but for whatever reason, the duo soon found themselves looking for personnel again. The men who would step up to the mark were guitarist John Frusciante, a long-time Peppers fan from their earliest shows (as Flea recalled it: "It seemed like a good idea at the time. When Hillel died, I asked John to join us. We had had a couple of jam sessions together. I knew he liked us and I knew he was a great guitarist") and drummer Chad Smith, a Harley Davidson-driving man's man who at first they considered rejecting for being "too rock".

This time the new band worked just fine. Honing a musical approach and an interpersonal relationship of rare quality at the same time, the foursome soon built a set of new songs of astonishing dexterity and power. The result was their best album to date, entitled *Mother's Milk* and released in 1989 to a barrage of positive reviews. High points included a cover of Stevie Wonder's "Higher Ground", the funk-fest "Nobody Weird Like Me" (featuring some of the fastest bass-slapping ever recorded from the jubilant Flea), and a lament for Slovak entitled "Knock Me Down"—"If you see me getting high, knock me down" sang Kiedis, plausibly—and the record's cover art, a beautiful young woman cradling the band in minature, has become one of the rock world's great pieces of art. All the facets of the Chilis were in place on *Mother's Milk*, with their heroes deified ("Magic Johnson"), their sexual urges expressed ("Sexy Mexican Maid"), and their influences revealed (the aforementioned rampant cover of Jimi Hendrix's "Fire"). To everyone's surprise—including the band's—"Higher Ground" actually became a radio hit, thanks largely to MTV, who played its video on high rotation. "Knock Me Down", a song with a bleak message but a funky rhythm, was also a hit. In early 1990 the album was certified gold—no mean feat coming from a band so close to personal tragedy and so new as a working unit.

As the new decade got underway, the Chilis were beginning to see the world in different terms. Kiedis, shaken to the foundation of his soul by the departure of his dear friend Slovak, had eschewed heroin—at least for a temporary period—and felt happier than he had in years, despite the seismic changes the band had been forced to endure. This led him to approach both his lyrics and his vocals in a more enlightened, visionary way. Flea, always the most extrovert Chili Pepper in musical terms, was beginning to wonder if his future might lie less in flurries of finger-pops and elaborate solos than with economy and subtlety. After all, the greatest funk bass players who ever lived—among them his idols Larry Graham and Bootsy Collins—were all aware of the value of sitting in a simple, groovy pocket as well as the virtues of lightning-speed dexterity. And Smith and Frusciante, finding their feet within the band and locking into a groove with the others like few musicians could, brought a rock-solid dependability and a definite classic pop sensibility— respectively—to the band. In particular, John's love of girl-group harmonies and the pure-pop template that had anchored so much sweet music from the Beatles to the Stones to the Temptations and back again made his contribution unique. A lover of herbal highs, he and Flea would share innumerable joints and make their music almost without thinking about it. As Flea later recalled, "Nothing's ever been conscious, especially not at that point, because we were pretty high most of the time. Even now, when we get together, there's never a discussion of what we're doing. We just close our eyes and start playing."

Admirable as this approach might seem today in the light of the current music scene's post-millennial return to garage-rock spontaneity—and admirable too, due to the studied dexterity which had typified and stultified the Chilis' earlier albums—it's more revealing than that. What the listener learns from seemingly flippant statements such as "we just close our eyes and start playing" from idealists such as Kiedis and Flea, is that a plateau had been reached by the band in 1990 and 1991 which offered them only one exit if they were to achieve all of which they were capable. To be the band they could truly be, the Red Hot Chili Peppers needed to create the album of their lives: one that would ring down the decades and make itself felt down the years as surely as an *Electric Ladyland* or a *Ziggy Stardust*.

Little did the Chilis, or anyone observing them, know that this album would be that very record. *Blood Sugar Sex Magik* was to be their finest moment (at least, from my perspective in 2005): a solid, real album that would unite their talents in a lasting way. Serendipitously, it seemed that the world of music needed just such an album. Musician and listener would meet at the right time and the right place at last.

Rather than hit up a fully functioning but fully sterile professional recording studio for the album which the Red Hot Chili Peppers knew would be their most important to date, the band put their heads together and evolved a plan which would push the envelope a long way. Once the decision had been made to work with producer Rick Rubin ("[because] he's a goat's-head worshipper—he's produced people like Slayer and Danzig," said Kiedis to the press, with a degree of sarcasm), the Chilis moved into an old house in LA's Laurel Canyon, a mansion which had once been a home for "wayward women" and was also owned in earlier years by Bugsy Siegel and WC Fields. The band referred to it as "Big House", with a degree of respect, after learning that it was supposedly haunted, and decking it out with flowers, posters, books, a vintage recording setup ("We used really old equipment," enthused Flea. "Our Neve board is from the Fifties") and of course instruments—including a grand piano, a toy grand piano and a didgeridoo. To make the experience all the more lasting, a camera crew was commissioned to film the recording of the album: the results ("It's not going to be a rockumentary," mocked Kiedis. "It's a *cockumentary*") were released on VHS the following year and on DVD at the end of the 1990s as *Funky Monks*. The film remains essential viewing for anyone interested in this period of the Chili Peppers' history.

As Frusciante recalled of the making of the album, "We didn't ever leave the place—you just woke up, relaxed, took a few deep breaths... and started making music. Very easy. Very beautiful. Concentrating on doing nothing. I don't really care about my own creativity. I didn't even pay attention to my own playing. I just care about my life. I wasn't even listening to the guitar or how I was making it sound during the recording sessions. I just enjoy playing music with people I love. You don't pay attention to what you're playing, you just look into the other guy's eyes, or at his hands, or his knee, or whatever."

The choice of Rubin as producer was key. Born Frederick Jay Rubin in suburban Long Island in 1963, he had grown up listening to classic rock bands such as Led Zeppelin and

AC/DC but was enthralled in his teens by the then-rising, New York-based hip-hop movement, which left him a devotee of both genres and the obvious person to work on bringing the two together. As a student at NYU in 1984, he founded the Def Jam record label with his friend Russell Simmons and immediately focused on bringing out hip-hop records, with notable first signings being LL Cool J (whose "I Need a Beat" was a hit) and Public Enemy, whose Rubin-produced debut album *Yo! Bum Rush the Show* appeared in 1987.

The key to Rubin's usefulness to the Chilis lies in his affinity with both hip-hop and rock. As well as all the hip-hop busting and rhyming, Rubin had found time to produce what remains one of the most extreme heavy metal albums of the decade, Slayer's *Reign In Blood*. Now acknowledged as the finest expression of the metal variant strand of the day—thrash metal—*Reign* was a horrifying fusillade of riffs and beats that was the polar opposite, stylistically, sonically, and thematically, of the hip-hop acts on the Def Jam roster. Perhaps it was only reasonable, then, that when he produced albums by the Beastie Boys (who had started life as a hardcore punk band) and Run-DMC, both acts would incorporate rock influences into their sound—in fact, the former band took this a stage further when they asked Slayer guitarist Kerry King to play a session for their international hit, "Fight For Your Right (To Party)".

Rubin saw the chance to work on aggressive music as just as useful an opportunity as the mellower material, saying, "People should be free to do whatever they want to do, and people should be free to listen to what they want to listen to. If someone makes something that you don't like, don't support it, don't listen to it." He expanded, "If you're for freedom of speech, you're against censorship. The same thing that will protect somebody fighting out against injustice protects the person saying something radically negative and terrible. You can't limit censorship to the things that you think are OK. You're either for it or you're against it. And if you're against it, everything goes. I don't think people should hurt other people, and I don't think that the influence of music is such that it does." Obviously referring to the Slayer albums he had worked on, among those of other acts, he added, "I've been involved with some very negative records that I'm proud of. I think that those records resonate with people who need to hear that energy, and I know that music doesn't cause people to go out and do bad things. I think if anything, it defuses them. There are a lot of people out there who are angry, and there's no reason that angry people can't be entertained as well as others. I think it's fine, I think it's a service. I think everybody should get to enjoy whatever it is that resonates with them."

Later on, however, the rock and rap obsessions that vied for Rubin's attentions caused the split of Def Jam, with Simmons retaining the old label (and finding much success as the hip-hop movement went global in the late 1980s) and Rick going on to found the Def American label in Los Angeles, where he signed Danzig, Masters of Reality, The Cult, Wolfsbane, and Slayer. Not that he abandoned his roots altogether—he also brought The Geto Boys to the public eye and continued to work with Public Enemy, LL Cool J and Run-DMC. He later branched out into activities such as wrestling, where he bought an entire circuit in the South.

Rubin's background was one that would serve any band—like the Chilis—who specialized in combining music styles, as he once explained: "I think, being suburban, there's less of a pretentiousness. I'll give you an example. I grew up an hour outside of Manhattan. One of the bands I worked with early on was the Beastie Boys, and their musical taste was radically different from mine. I liked bands like AC/DC, Led Zeppelin—they hated those things. Because being cool kids in the city, those things were too commercial, too mainstream. So the Beastie Boys liked really underground stuff, which served them well. It was cool, and it made them who they were. But I think it was the collaboration between my more suburban, mainstream taste and their more eclectic, underground taste that made our working together so successful.

"Growing up, I always wished I lived in the city, instead of on the Island, but, in retrospect, I learned a lot about the culture that I wouldn't have learned had I grown up in Manhattan. I feel like I had the best of both worlds because I was close enough to be in the city, but far enough away that I didn't have what I'll call a 'holier than thou' attitude. It's not that I don't like those things, but I'm not bound by those things."

By the time that Rubin's path crossed that of the Red Hot Chili Peppers, he had found both critical and commercial success, with a whole new rise in music—then naively known as rap-rock or rap-metal, later the more generic nu-metal—on the rise. This was due more or less to a single record, 1987's Aerosmith and Run-DMC collaboration on a version of the former's earlier hit "Walk This Way". The song had relaunched Aerosmith's dormant career and instilled in hip-hop and heavy metal fans—who had been eyeing each other across the cultural divide with a degree of mutual respect since the early 1980s—an awareness that the two could be successfully combined. Of "Walk This Way", Rubin shrugged, "It didn't seem, for me, as unusual as it did for other people. I grew up with rap music and with rock music, and they always felt like different versions of the same thing to me. People viewed them as such polar opposites: I can't tell you how many times people have talked to me about rap not being music. But if you listen to [the original version of] "Walk This Way" by Aerosmith, it really is not that different from rap. It shares a lot."

So what skills did Rick Rubin bring to the table when he was assigned to work with the Chili Peppers? The whole package, as he explained, "I don't feel that my job is done once the music is finished; it can also be my job to be involved in other aspects of what a band does. Depending on the band, I'm often involved in artwork and videos, marketing approaches—how people perceive the band. It's continuing on with a project instead of just passing it off." Of his modus operandi as a producer, he explained, "In working with a band, I find what's good about them and help bring it out. Also, songs are a big deal for me. I'd say that my biggest contribution to bands is helping them get their material together. I know that some producers are more concerned about what it sounds like. And I'm clearly involved in what it sounds like, but it's almost more like I join a band when I produce a record. But, I'm unlike all the other members of the band, who each have their own personal agenda. The bass player is concerned about the bass part; everyone is concerned about their own part. I'm the only member of the band that doesn't care about any of those particulars. I just care that the whole thing is as good as it can be. I want to say it's less about the details, although it's all about the details, so that's not quite right. But it is a grander vision."

What was it that had attracted him to the Chilis? Something must have clicked, of course, as at one stage his Def American label had been a contender to sign them in the bout of pre-*Blood Sugar Sex Magik* competition which the giant Warner Brothers label had ultimately won. "It's really about falling in love," he said. "I'm not looking for any type of anything or to fit any mould. I'm not looking for the next Prince or something. It's really an emotional connection that transcends any genre. Just listen to feelings. You just know. You don't even have to think about it. When you listen to music you know what you like and what you don't… Some of the things that I love the best when I first heard them, I laughed at them and thought that they were crazy. I remember when I first heard The Ramones; I just laughed. I thought they were ridiculous, and they became one of my favorite groups. When something is revolutionary, it's hard on first listen to accept it. There's a shocking period there, where you don't know. A lot of the things that you hear once and you love may fade faster… sometimes it's the stuff that takes a little while to get around before you realize how good it is that really stays with you. Because that's the stuff that's different."

Rubin had gained a reputation for being difficult on various records, but this was inaccurate, it seemed. "It probably was a device to survive life, more than being a gimmick to present an image. It was probably just to live in the world and be OK…" he laughed at one point. "There's nothing better than telling the truth. When I start working with a band, I explain, 'Look, I'm just going to tell you everything I think. I'm telling you that, not in any way to criticize what you do, but to do my job.' And they can listen to what I say, accept it and try it, or they can say, 'You know what? What you don't like about this is what I like about it. Fuck you, it's fine'... I have a strong opinion and I explain it clearly. Actually, the way I got started making records was going out to hip-hop clubs in the early 1980s, then hearing the rap records that came out that sounded nothing like what was going on in the clubs. I was a fan of what was really going on, who went out and got all these records and none of them sounded like they were supposed to... I was really just a fan wanting to chronicle what I went out and heard. I never thought this would be a job. I always liked music, but it never seemed like a way to support yourself."

When the Laurel Canyon sessions came round with the Chili Peppers, the band had evidently put in some time on pre-production—the time in which songs are rehearsed, arranged and finalized—as the recording went smoothly from day one. This was a central tenet of Rick Rubin's production approach, as he explained, "It's the pre-production time that really makes the difference. Sometimes that's a couple of weeks, sometimes it's a few months, sometimes it's a year of getting ready to go into the studio and cut the whole album in a week. The preference is always to get as much done before you go in the studio as possible." The producer had a self-confessed dislike for extended studio sessions: "I don't love it. The idea of knowing how it can be is the best part. And then the actual work of having to get it

31

there is just going through the process. Once you hear it in your head, it's like being a carpenter—trying to build the thing when you already know what it is. The fun part is knowing what it is. But no one else gets to know what it is unless you do the work."

Would that work produce the expected results?

Recent polls in music magazines have shown time and time again that the average, modern-day, rock-music-consuming listener—which is to say a man (frequently a woman, but usually a man) aged between 12 and 40—loves the 1990s. While the 1960s is the decade which most music-savvy people nominate as the greatest decade of them all in music terms, it's the 1990s—derided at the time for its cheesy rave music, its recycled Britpop and its lumbering stadium-rock dinosaurs—that usually comes up second. When you stop and think about it, this makes sense.

Flea said it best in *Rolling Stone* magazine in 1992. "The world at large is just completely bored with mainstream bullshit. They want something that not only has a hardcore edge but that is real music, written by real people who wake up and have the unignorable need to create music." When he referred to 'mainstream bullshit', it seems that he was referring to any big-selling band not fortunate enough to be in the alternative rock club in the wake of the rise of grunge, the movement which took the modern music scene by the throat and made it aware of its own failings.

At the end of the 1980s, in many ways the gaudiest and most ludicrous decade in music to date, West Coast America wasn't producing any bands big enough or original enough for many people to take notice. In the UK a sea-change had come with the Manchester scene focusing on the Happy Mondays, the Stone Roses and the Inspiral Carpets, but in the US this had not registered significantly and all eyes, where people bothered to look, were focused on black music. At the turn of the decade, the shocking new music coming out of California and New York—the two poles of American creativity, then as now—was hip-hop. In 1991 alone, landscape-changing albums appeared from Public Enemy (*Fear Of A Black Planet*), LL Cool J (*Mama Said Knock You Out*), A Tribe Called Quest (*People's Instinctive Travels By Paths And Rhythms*), and Ice Cube (*AmeriKKKa's Most Wanted*). Even UK acts such as Soul II Soul (*Vol. II: 1990, A New Decade*) and Massive Attack (*Blue Lines*) made their mark on the hip-hop scene that year. Add to this the enduring impact of late-1980s records from Ice-T, Schoolly D, and the infamous NWA (soon to spawn the talented Dr Dre) and it's clear that hip-hop was where it was at.

Now, apply this situation to a band such as the Red Hot Chili Peppers—fiercely fond of funk and weaned on the coolest jazz—and you have a recipe for inspiration. Urged by a *Rolling Stone* interviewer to pass comment on a contemporary rock band called Ugly Kid Joe—who had enjoyed a brief moment in the sun with a hit entitled "Everything About You" but then quickly fell from grace—Flea responded with the terse words: "Our music is so much heavier than that... I just know where their music is coming from—copping us, copping Faith No More, copping Pop-Rock Band No. 17B. We're coming from listening to Miles Davis, Ornette Coleman, Defunkt, Funkadelic, The Meters, James Brown—

the real shit. And it's coming from jamming and playing a billion hours of shit that no one will hear; getting cosmic in a darkened room and developing music telepathy."

"Real" when the term meant something, the Chilis' modus operandi was about sucking the marrow of groove from the bones of music and turning it into something new and meaningful rather than a contrived take on someone else's idea. "All we ever want to do is play music that comes from our hearts," Flea insisted. "All the other shit comes from having fun. Like me and Hillel and Anthony used to live together in this house. People would come over, we'd hang out, smoke pot and drink beer, put socks on our dicks and run around. It was kids living together, having fun."

The fun he referred to stemmed in part from the anything-goes vibe of the music scene at the time, especially prevalent in the liberal environment in which the band found themselves and not limited to any one sole style or method. Together with the band's determination to sink into the groove, serve the song without resorting to simple dexterity and produce something genuine, the creative opportunity of the day provided a nurturing atmosphere into which something special had to be born.

The radio waves reverberated at the time with classic music that has now been acknowledged for its inventiveness. When it came to mainstream music, albums from Sinéad O'Connor (*I Do Not Want What I Haven't Got*), the Pet Shop Boys (*Behavior*), Depeche Mode (*Violator*), George Michael (*Listen Without Prejudice Vol. 1*), Garth Brooks (*No Fences*), The Black Crowes (*Shake Your Money Maker*), Paul Simon (*The Rhythm Of The Saints*), and Prince (*Graffiti Bridge*)—for better or for worse—shaped the sounds of the masses with stripped-down rock, an increasing dose of electronic experimentation and a remarkably diverse palette of sounds. Old stagers such as Neil Young & Crazy Horse, and Lou Reed & John Cale (*Ragged Glory* and *Songs For Drella* respectively) were also still doing the rounds and more or less retaining their dignity.

Bands which would shortly become known as 'alternative rock' (and later still "alt.rock", as the internet and newgroups expanded) were in the ascendant. Faith No More, in many ways the Chilis' closest contemporaries, were riding high in the wake of a career-best album, *The Real Thing*, while records also came thick and fast from Jane's Addiction (*Ritual De Lo Habitual*), the Breeders (*Pod*), Sonic Youth (*Goo*), the Pixies (*Bossanova*), and Fugazi (*Repeater*). Overseas acts of the same unclassifiable ilk such as Nick Cave And The Bad Seeds (*The Good Son*), the Cocteau Twins (*Heaven Or Las Vegas*), The Sundays (*Reading, Writing And Arithmetic*), Ride (*Nowhere*), Prefab Sprout (*Jordan: The Comeback*), The La's (*The La's*), and World Party (*Goodbye Jumbo*) also delivered work that nowadays reads like a who's-who of non-mainstream music. As for heavy metal and its offshoots, Living Colour stood alone in a field of one— black, political-commentary funk-metal—with their excellent *Time's Up*, and Slayer unleashed a fusillade of thrash metal with *Seasons In The Abyss*, which surprised pundits by attracting exposure on MTV. The dance music explosion was yet to come—with its techno and ambient strands still subjugated by hip-hop—but landmark albums such as The KLF's *Chill Out* and Deee-Lite's *World Clique* were much praised nonetheless.

It was in this atmosphere of extreme artistic tension that *Blood Sugar Sex Magik* was recorded.

the players

The boys with the skills to pay the bills

Blood Sugar Sex Magik was such a landmark in the career of the Red Hot Chili Peppers because it was the perfect expression of the band themselves. They had finally hit their stride, developed an almost telepathic understanding of the art they were creating (in particular, Frusciante and Flea were a melodic team to die for) and grown into mature songwriters. And yet the band were still perceived as a funk-rock, or worse, a funk-metal, act, despite the marvelous array of influences that had come to bear fruit.

So who are these funky monks anyway? Let's start with the walking hard-on himself...

Anthony Kiedis (vocals)

"When we started fusing funk and rock, we never intended to spearhead a movement," said Anthony Kiedis. "It's not as though we're the first to mix funk and rock. Long before us there was Sly Stone and Parliament-Funkadelic. At the early shows, people used to say, 'you guys are really into P-Funk, right?' At that point, we hadn't heard that stuff. But then we really got into it, and eventually we got George Clinton to produce the second album, *Freaky Styley*." The frontman's perception of the energy behind various styles of music was profound, when he discussed hip-hop ("We're not against music that depends on technology... It's just that we prefer to be an all-live, hands-on band. But my favorite band is Public Enemy and they use samplers and drum machines. There's a lot of rap music that's ridiculously funky"), house music ("it's the most blasphemous, soulless, cold-blooded noise I ever heard"), and even the LA music *du jour* at the time of the album, thrash metal, headed up at the time by Rubin's old friends Slayer ("That kind of ferocity is one-dimensional: it's very male music, but without any sexual energy").

Kiedis is a character with depth. His childhood was an unusual one, mentored principally by his father, the actor Blackie Dammett. After a childhood spent living with his mother in Michigan, Kiedis moved to LA at the age of 11. Assisted by his father, he appeared in one or two films under the name Cole Dammett (as he recalled of his bit-part as Sylvester Stallone's son in the 1978 film *F.I.S.T.*, "I had one line. It was, 'pass the milk,' and I think you can just see my arm in the frame as I say it...") but later focused solely on music.

Dammett, who his son affectionately described once as "your basic semisubversive underground hooligan playboy womanizer type of character," was a positive, if also unorthodox role model for Anthony. As the singer recalled, "He was not your nine-to-fiver, and he definitely had a strong influence on me. He was very supportive of my personal education and my creative development... My father had a constant turnover of girlfriends. It wasn't that he was this cold-hearted user of people. He just had this insatiable desire to meet all the beautiful girls in the world. That was great because I got to develop this early self-confidence with women... Fortunately, I had enough of my mother's genuineness in me. At a pretty early age I fell in love with a girl and stayed with her for three years. So it wasn't like I was destined to do the same thing my father was doing. At the same time, I thought it was the greatest thing in the world to have all these beautiful women come into my house and not be uptight about me hanging out with them and having sex with them. You can believe my friends were rather impressed with my situation."

He later recalled a trip with Dammett accompanied by several suitcases full of marijuana, which his father was smuggling. "He [Dammett] was thinking that I was a good beard. Being seen with a kid defused any criminal suspicions that law enforcement might have had. That's a pretty good grift, having a little kid with you while you're doing something illegal. It would be like, oh, that's a father and son, there certainly can't be a hundred pounds of weed in those suitcases... He and I were constantly at risk, from age six when I would come to visit and they would be doing giant dope deals out of [his house in] Topanga. I'd be in the house and there would be piles of drugs and piles of money and piles of people. But he must have thought it was OK. He was willing personally to take the chance with his own life. And he must have felt that whatever happened, I would be OK... It was good training for life, being thrown into a crisis and having to be quick on your feet."

Sex entered the young Kiedis's life at an early stage, helped along by Dammett and his California lifestyle, which Anthony enjoyed at first sight. "I completely embraced it. The whole picture out here was just a natural high—the costumes that people were wearing, the music that people were playing, the art that people were making—I loved it.

The first time I smoked pot, I was with my dad, and to me, it just seemed like I'd landed in this magical kingdom where anything was possible. I got stoned, and my father had a girl over at the house, and she didn't have her shirt on. I said to myself, you know, 'How lucky could a boy be?' At the time, I thought I was the luckiest kid on the block." The early Chilis albums, up to and including *Blood Sugar Sex Magik*, are full of sexual references—but always imbued with a pure, non-lecherous, non-destructive air that seems to stem directly from the LA life that the singer led as a child.

Kiedis is also a sensitive individual, falling head over heels with the singer Sinéad O'Connor at one point. "I made an ass of myself by being so incredibly infatuated at a certain point," he mused later. "That infatuation works to a degree and inspired me to write all this stuff that I would give to her, but it was an overload of diabolical romantic strangeness. It culminated with this thing of going to the Academy Awards—I wanted to go with her and she ended up going with Daniel Day-Lewis. Then she just skipped town. It was very abrupt. When I ran into her years later, and I saw her in the back of a limousine with Peter Gabriel, I looked at her and she looked at me: I said hello, she smiled real big and acted like nothing ever happened. OK, if she wanted to act that way then I'd have to just let it be. She's just prone to being unpredictable. Crazy. I loved all of her antics; everyone should have a voice to say whatever the fuck they want to say." He also enjoyed a dalliance with actor and director Sofia Coppola. "She's got a certain brand of cool that can't be matched. She's super-smart and different. Her demeanor was not typical in any way. She lived in an artistic way. Coming from her background, the way she went about working and being a person seemed honorable and beautiful to me. She has a quietness about her that's appealing. We were approaching coupledom status when it fell off the rails. This was years before she became a director."

Drugs were an early part of his life. An early acid experience enthralled him: "We [a friend and I] were so welcoming to that experience. I read about LSD and I never looked forward to trying a drug as much as I did with LSD. I was consumed with the idea of experiencing that type of altered consciousness—whether it was heroin, peyote or LSD. The acid we got was very pure. We took one trip in Bel-Air and got the suburban LA thing. We took another down in Mexico where we stayed in the ocean for eight hours. It was fantastic. No fear, no trepidation…"

He also explained of the chemical effects of cocaine and heroin: "They're polar opposites, which makes them go perfectly together. I've never understood why most people don't get that. Cocaine is a bummer without heroin. I've met hundreds of addicts who only take cocaine, and I wondered how they lived through all the miserable come-downs. One releases all the serotonin in your brain, and the other releases all the dopamine. These are two very euphoric chemicals. One [cocaine] flashes in a pan and then leaves you deleted, and one [heroin] keeps releasing until you become completely strung out. So you really need both. It was described to me by a doctor that cocaine releases the chemical in your brain that is associated with listening to rhythmic music, where you want to get up and dance, like with James Brown, and heroin releases the same chemical that is released when you hear beautiful melody, which makes tears come from your eyes. Sometimes you want to dance, sometimes you want that emotional connection. It was just a fluke that I stumbled into the fact that they go well together."

As for Kiedis's later spiral into drug addiction, he mused, "As far as the drug thing goes, I don't regret anything in that area, because it got me where I am today, and I'm cool with that. But it definitely introduced a struggle into my life. Having no limits, I had to personally determine what I was capable of doing and what would bring me to an early grave. It took me a long time, and I lost friends along the way, but now I know from first-hand experience."

Kiedis described himself at the height of his addiction as "withering away, mentally, spiritually, physically, creatively—everything was fading out," explaining, "I reached a point where I could not do it any more. It wasn't working. I wasn't able to escape, no matter how much I put in my body. I could not get away. I called someone and said, 'I don't know what to do. I can't get high. I can't stay sober.' That's when I got shipped off to a rehab." But his recovery was temporary, and he slipped back into drug use: "I didn't realize how much work it took to create a psychic change sufficient to maintain sobriety. I fooled myself into thinking, if I can stay sober for a month, I'm good. It's an experience of daily maintenance. It's principles to live by. You can't do it for a little while and then go back to not maintaining your condition and think that you're going to stay sober."

In 2004 he published an autobiography, *Scar Tissue*, and in it wrote that not a week would pass without the urge to get high. "It's true," he explained to *Playboy*. "It's going to sound worse to the normie than to the person who's in recovery. It's not a problem. It's a pretty healthy fear to have. I don't become obsessed with the thought. It doesn't have a physical power over me. When you're strung out and you don't use for a while, you get obsessed with the idea of using and you have a physical reaction: a stomach ache, your bowels churn, you get nervous, your hair stands on end, your skin crawls. You have to have it, your body demands it. That does not happen to me. When I get a thought it's intentional, letting me know it's still who I am. It's not tormenting, it's very comfortable... I'm not a fan of antidepressants. Depression is a part of life. It's not the worst thing in the world. Find a way to accept that emotion and do something other than take a fucking pill to deal with it, like changing your lifestyle or going to any length to get well, without taking a psychotropic drug. That makes more sense than taking a pill to alter your chemistry. That's a Band-Aid. You're just fucking with your head's chemistry even worse. It's a real cop-out by the medical profession and the pharmaceutical industry."

Clearly only a person who had taken such a journey could write a song like "Under The Bridge" with any genuine verisimilitude—and perhaps in such vague terms. As the singer laughed, many of those who bought the song for its simple, sweet qualities were unaware of its broader connotation and might be in for a surprise when they explored the wider Chilis canon: "What kills me is that there are so many people getting into 'Under The Bridge' across America who have no idea what the Chili Peppers are like. Take a group of Kansas housewives who turn on the radio and say: 'Oh, I like that sweet, sentimental song. Honey would you go out and get me this record?' They get the record, and there's 'Sir Psycho Sexy' and 'The Power of Equality'. They are going to have their little world turned upside down... I have this wonderful image of this lady washing the dishes in her little home in Kansas with her little tape deck, popping this in and taking off her clothing, running into the back yard and getting loosened up a bit."

Why should sex be such a powerful element of Kiedis's songwriting? No reason, apparently, other than because it exists in the first place, as he told the press: "It seems like perfect material for art, like death and every other fundamental aspect of existence. It's right up there with the biggies as far as I can tell." But this artistic perceptiveness may mask a more jovial side than the one he reveals to the media. As drummer Chad Smith said of him with affection, "He's usually on the make... it's beyond the usual rock-star-cliché thing. He really fancies himself a connoisseur of women."

Not that he was much of a connoisseur when the infamous socks-on-cocks stunt was first performed, as he once explained. As an 18-year-old UCLA political science student, he recalled that a fellow student was making unwanted advances: "I wasn't really into her," he explained, "but she would send me these cards with foldout cocks, with the yardstick on it." On her arrival one day, Kiedis came to meet her adorned only in a sock: "Not just over the cock, but over the cock and balls," he added. "It was just a gag. And it was a good gag." The sock gag debuted professionally at a Chilis show at a Hollywood strip bar called the Kit Kat. "Since it was a strip club, we decided to come out for the encore with the socks," said Kiedis. "And brother, let me tell you, when we came out of the little dressing room backstage, we were levitating with nervous energy. I could not find my feet on the stage. And somebody filmed it. I don't know if the film still exists, but we saw it, and we just had this look in our eyes like we were from outer space."

One might expect, with all of Kiedis's lack of reservations when it comes to singing or speaking about controversial subjects—and in America, so much these days is controversial, even if you're not the frontman of a sex-obsessed, nudity-loving rock band—that he would be an outspoken, extroverted character. Surprisingly, this appears not to be the case, with the singer coming across as shy, quiet, or more often coldly detached in the thousands of interviews he has conducted over the decades. Perhaps this introspective nature explains his desire to express himself in this most expressive of bands, and also the struggle with heroin—the most inward-looking and exterior-defocusing of all drugs—which has plagued him since his teens. But there's a core of humanity there, with his sense of humor depending on his feelings at any given moment, as he explained: "I guess it depends on the mood I'm in. We're just coming from the viewpoint of being alive at a time of such a preposterous media reality. You have to be willing to laugh at yourself and recognize what's coming from a real place and what's coming from an empty place. Obviously we go in both directions, and we've found ourselves getting ridiculous. It's more important to us to just make music and play it and not to worry about that stuff. We're not big image-makers and we're not trying to put media spins out to the world. We're a pretty simple band, basically, kind of an old-fashioned band, that plays the best we can and puts on a good show."

Therapy, drug recovery, and good old-fashioned hard knocks seem to have given Kiedis a healthy self-awareness, as he revealed when explaining of his music—as only the more enlightened of us ever can—that sometimes, it's human not to be able to see the woods for the trees: "While we were making this record, we were too involved with it to really get the overview," he said. "But when I listen to it now, a lot of the material is just pure—in love with love, and in love with nature, and in love with the fact that we're doing exactly what we want to do. And a lot of that love is inspired by being depressed, being lonely and being heartbroken. That's the reason why I listen to music—to connect emotionally with all these different things."

Emotions, the buzzword for the modern, post-therapy, post-*Iron John* man, are at the forefront of Kiedis's mind at all times: "As much as it is to stimulate my intellect, it's really to stimulate a spectrum of emotions. There was never an intention. There's an element to our band that's just a series of accidents and mistakes and mishaps and experiments which just turned into something that works." And times have been hard in Kiedis's life, despite the fortune which has beamed on him and his band since the impact of *Blood Sugar Sex Magik*—one of the worst moments occurring when his early cohorts Hillel Slovak and drummer Jack Irons left to join What Is This before the Chilis had even recorded their first album: "I was left there sobbing, thinking, well, there goes my plan to conquer the world. But six hours later we regrouped and said, OK, we can't let this die now."

In later years, after his band had gone on to conquer the world a second time, Kiedis's icy exterior melted somewhat and he was able to express himself a little better. "I feel like a new band," he said. "When we get together to rehearse, we could write music together all day long—good music."

"Anthony's changed like crazy," Frusciante would add of the newly expressive frontman. "He realizes the power he has to hurt people or to nurture them. Before, you never knew—one day he was your friend, the next day he wasn't "

John Frusciante (guitar)

"I still think that John was the missing link," said Flea. "Only with him were we able to create an album like *Blood Sugar Sex Magik*."

The most troubled member of the Chili Peppers of all—Kiedis's bizarre upbringing and drug problems, and Flea's troubled youth notwithstanding—is the talented John Frusciante, who would spiral down into a near-fatal drug haze in subsequent years but who at the time of recording *Blood Sugar Sex Magik* was merely an intense young man struggling with the pressures of fame and success. Much later in life, after enduring tortures that would fell anyone else, he added: "I've always believed that music is something that can't be expressed using words. I remember being at a baseball game when I was a kid. I was trying to play, and failing miserably, as usual. I was very angry and frustrated, so I just stood in the outfield and wrote a song in my head. Then I went home and filled a whole side of a tape with songs I made up. I was very angry back then. I don't need to express those kinds of emotions now, but I'm still a firm believer that music isn't something you can express with words."

Frusciante once laughed at the idea of music being reducible to pure data: "I don't think that music is just little notes. Music is energy, and energy is the single most important form of it in the world. Without energy, there is no life. The only difference between a dead person and a live person is the energy, the electricity flowing inside their system, and that's what makes music. You can't make a good record with people who have no life inside them and people who are totally bored just playing the notes. Yeah, the Velvet Underground could have taught four fucking businessmen who knew how to play instruments their songs, and they would have played the same fucking notes, but would it have been the same music? Fuck, no. It would have been crap. Music is what it is because of the energy.

"If I feel totally drab one day, and I try to record a song, and then I feel totally alive another day and I try to record the same song, the one that I recorded when I had the life flowing through me is going to be the one that's good. There was a time in my life where my energy was not flowing right inside me. I knew, technically, how to put notes together and how to put chords together to make songs. To write a song, you need to have a flow of energy from the second you get the idea until the song is finished. Your energy has to be flowing. You have to have a feeling inside, and you have to grab a hold of that feeling, and you don't let go of it until the song is finished. At the time that my energy wasn't flowing right inside me, I was incapable of doing that. If I had an idea for a song, yeah I could start it, but it just tended to go off in nothingness, and it started to drift and drift until I lost interest in doing it and I couldn't really find anywhere interesting to go. You have to have a lot of energy to write music, and that's what the music is."

He went on, "The notes are the least important part of music. There's a lot of great music that doesn't even have notes, but the people that make it are people of great personal power and personal conviction and people who life means something to... The notes don't matter at all. Aside from notes, you have to remember that it's a combination of rhythm, notes and texture. Music is not just notes. Rhythm, notes and texture. The notes have a correlation to the way that life goes up and down and the notes go up and down. Inwardly we go up and down, and notes go up and down. That's what they mean to us. When you put chords behind it, it starts to work into appealing to your subconscious in a way that expresses things that we can't intellectually express."

Frusciante's destiny was—to him at least—apparent from a young age, as he later recalled: "I knew that I was gonna be a guitarist ever since I can remember: there were voices in my head that were telling me so." As it had for the other Chilis, punk rock honed his vision and freed him from the restrictions of conventional musical study: "The Germs' first show made me realize that being good at the guitar wasn't something you had to work at... As long as you put the right kind of energy and feeling into your playing, that was what mattered. Then one day I was feeling a lot of rage—I was angry at two kids that I didn't like and didn't like me—so I went home and wrote 30 short punk songs in a row on my acoustic guitar. That was the first day that I really started playing."

Frusciante added: "When I first heard The Germs, I had had all these feelings of rage inside of me, and I didn't know how to express anything, and then all of a sudden there was this music that totally calms my brain, that totally soothes my brain. I don't even understand what's taking place inside of my brain or why I'm so confused. All I know is that when I hear The Germs, I'm not confused any more. Don't ever let anybody tell you music is stupid. Fucking assholes!"

As he explained, all music was just as important: "The music I thought I was supposed to be listening to didn't really give me the same feeling as David Bowie, the New York Dolls and T.Rex... listening to those bands and getting experience through jamming was pretty much where I was at when I joined the Chili Peppers."

Transfixed as a youth by the sounds of the new wave (Martha & The Muffins), hard rock (AC/DC, Kiss), and punk (The Germs), Frusciante later claimed to be playing the Sex Pistols' *Never Mind The Bollocks* album on his grandfather's acoustic guitar by the age of ten. Later on, he auditioned for Frank Zappa's band (but "chickened out" after waiting in line, as he later recalled). After a stint at guitar school John saw the Chilis play at a 1985 show at LA's Variety Arts Center: he struck up a friendship with Hillel Slovak and the rest is history, other than to observe that his very first band—even before the Chilis—was a brief stint alongside Flea in the coulda-beens (and never-weres) Thelonius Monster.

As we noted earlier, John had joined a band that he idolized, meaning that his perceptions of his bandmates were based not on reality but on hero worship—not a healthy working relationship for anyone, even for those equipped with the strongest mind. He explained how his vision of the band didn't gel with the stadium beast that they became after *Blood Sugar Sex Magik*. "When I was 17 and I was at the last Chili Peppers show I ever saw before joining them, Hillel asked me,

'Would you still like the Chilis if they got so popular they played the LA Forum?' I said, 'No. It would ruin the whole thing that's great about the band. The audience feels no different from the band at all.' There was this real kind of historical vibe at their shows, none of the frustration that runs through the audience when they jump around and can't get out of their seat. I didn't even watch the shows. I'd get so excited that I'd flip around the slam pit the whole time. I really felt like a part of the band, and all the sensitive people in the audience did, too. So I couldn't picture the band playing the LA Forum, and when we got to that point of popularity it bugged me for that and a number of other reasons."

But this seems hardly sufficient to explain Frusciante's deeper, darker malaise. What was the cause of all this inner turmoil? John has never been specific about what fuelled his later breakdown, telling one interviewer, "It's subconscious childhood pain which you've pushed into your memory and then suddenly it pops out 20 years later and you're a drug addict... to have childhood pain you don't need an unhappy childhood. It can be one little moment... or a period of a couple of weeks that ends up growing... or 10 minutes in a couple of weeks that can have a profound effect on the rest of your life." Apparently he was a contented child—despite the divorce of his parents when he was six—and translated this to his early work with the Chili Peppers, visibly animated with enjoyment during the recording of *Blood Sugar Sex Magik* and known for his joyful participation in rehearsals. "At rehearsals I would be jumping around, because you get ideas while you're doing it that you never get otherwise. It's a way of hearing things that you wouldn't normally hear... I don't really think very much in terms of words, but I use my brain a lot for colors and for music, and it's important to be at the receptive end of music as opposed to feeling like it is your responsibility to be creating it all of the time. The feeling of absorbing music is a lot more important."

It's clearly a source of immense support to Frusciante that his band are as close, or closer, than brothers to him. "Luckily, I'm in a band with people who love me being the way I am. Nobody expects me to act in a way that I don't feel like acting... A lot of times when I'm dancing, it's to try and show things about the space that I'm hearing in the music and how one point connects to another. I'm dancing in a musical way, to try to figure things out." The connection he felt to those closest to him—so intense as to be spiritual, or even telepathic—has always featured heavily in interviews he has given to the press.

For example, the bond he shared with the late actor and musician River Phoenix—who would die of a speedball overdose two years after the recording of BSSM—was profound. "Me and River used to play together. We had a sort of communication that was intense, on just two guitars. We did two songs. One's called 'Bought Her Soul'... I recorded the song and I said to River, 'Make sounds with your voice and I'll record you backwards over this song but you're not allowed to hear the song.' So he made sounds into the mic while I recorded and listened to it on the headphones. That's the other voice in the background besides my voice. It went perfectly with the song. We were cosmic together... The other song is 'Soul Removal'. He sings and wrote the first half, and I wrote the second half, and you can hear the guitars on that. It has the thickness of a bunch of guitars, but the unity of one guitar.

We weave in and out of each other in a really cool, natural way."

The music they made was inspired, Frusciante clarified, by another famous social misfit and drug casualty: "Syd Barrett [original Pink Floyd leader] really inspired that song. I was thinking about him a lot at that time... the three major influences on [me] are Syd Barrett, Robert Johnson, and Captain Beefheart." (Flea also knew Phoenix, and wrote a later song, "Transcending", for him. "It's about one of the kindest people I ever met in my life," he said. "When I think about River I don't think about his death. I don't get sad about it. I think about how incredibly fortunate I was to be friends with a person who looked inside me and saw things that no one else ever saw before. And that song is a respectfully loving song for him.")

Perhaps Frusciante's most obvious and celebrated partnership is the one he shares with Flea. Sharing most of the *Blood Sugar Sex Magik* composition with the bassist ("I wrote like, 60 percent of the music and Flea wrote 40," he said), he loved the recording sessions for the album with a passion: "Yeah, I had a good time," he smiled, "because I was always looking at Flea and my amp." The pair had a side-project in progress too, he explained. "Me and Flea and [Jane's Addiction/Porno For Pyros drummer] Steven Perkins have a band. We're called the Three Amoebas. We have ten or 15 hours of stuff on tape, and it's great. There are never any dull moments ... it all fucking flows perfectly. It doesn't have any of the things that made instrumental rock laughable a few years down the line. So we're gonna release that, and they're the main people I'm interested in jamming with. Me and Flea jam now and then, but Steven's really busy with Porno right now. I don't really know any other musicians."

Asked about his influences, he mused, "Hendrix has had the biggest effect on the way I look at music. To me there's no difference between him and Igor Stravinsky, or Edgard Varese, or Iannis Xenakis, or John Coltrane, or Miles Davis, or Eric Dolphy, because music is one big cosmic swirl of beauty. It's just all God. It's not like people who are great musicians are separate entities. I think they're all one. Right now I feel like I'm doing something that's really worthwhile for the world, which is playing some of the most groundbreaking music of all time in the Red Hot Chili Peppers. And to me, when you have that sort of beauty in your life, goals aren't necessary."

In the early days he also talked about discipline—perhaps in ways that some might not have expected. "About a month ago Anthony and I went ten days without having an orgasm… we weren't allowed to masturbate or anything. In fact, right when we decided to go ten days without an orgasm, opportunity knocked, and we had to really hold back. And as far as my music, it isn't a matter of discipline in the sense that I'm being forced to do something I don't wanna do. It just comes very naturally out of an unconditional love for something. That's true discipline."

But most notably, Frusciante is a man whose inner visions are as important to him as anything that goes on outside him. This tendency would make him prone to post-rehab psychobabble in later years but, at the time of recording *BSSM*, he was simply in the habit of talking about existence on different planes and dimensions. "My whole object as a musician—no matter who I'm playing with—is to get as far away from myself as possible," he once explained. "The further I am away from the situation, the better the music is.

I feel like I'm letting the air play with me, and the air makes the music and I'm just an outline within that. The air that surrounds me is the actual walking person and this bit of flesh in between is just a blob...

"Did you ever try to disappear, actually to be in another universe, when you shut your eyes? I used to do things onstage to trick myself. Like tell myself I'm gonna start this solo on this fret note, then when it gets to the last second I'm not allowed to get to that fret, and I have to start somewhere else. Or I'll tell the audience that this song is dedicated to the baby born right now. But when it gets to the solo, the audience thinks they're thinking about the same baby as me but we're really thinking of two different babies. That kinda thing. You have to make fun of yourself. I'd just think it was a joke whatever I played, like what I played was ridiculous, and they'd go, 'That was so beautiful', what I'd just played for [Blood Sugar Sex Magik]. And I'd just think it was full of shit."

In fact, it emerged that as soon as he had finished tracking his parts for the album, Frusciante was considering leaving—despite the enormous and important tour that the band had lined up for the rest of 1991 and some of 1992: "I had a weird premonition that I should quit immediately after I finished my guitar parts... I'd say to myself, 'I know you don't have any reason to, but you've gotta quit the band.' But I couldn't bring myself to do it, because I knew they [the other bandmembers] wouldn't let me. It wouldn't make sense to them. But I had this feeling that the road was really gonna fuck with me. The road had been fucking with Flea for so many years, and it would have been bad of me to have quit then, but I was sure I should do it."

Add to this a certain discomfort he felt with the all-jumping, all-gurning, all-crazy band the Chilis were at this point, and it's little wonder the guitarist felt under pressure to seek out some freedom. "At that time I think everyone in the band felt like it was their job to jump around and make funny faces," he said. "I definitely had a problem being in a band like that... Flea was actually the one who told me back when I was first in the band that his favorite guitarists were the ones who were really mellow and didn't jump around."

Asked how he had first decided to become a rock musician, he explained, "Well, it was put to me by 'that guy' [his name for an internal voice which he regards as a kind of guardian spirit] when I was, like, four. So I went into my parents' record collection and found a rock 'n' roll compilation. And when my mom asked if I wanted to move to LA, I said, 'Yeah,' because I knew that was where the rock stars were. I was seven. Then when I found punk and listened to The Germs, I started seeing how I was part of this. I remember being out on the baseball field when I was 11, and I felt like such an outsider. Standing there in right field, I started making up an angry punk song in my head, and I went home and wrote, like, 20 songs in a row. I realized it didn't even matter if I knew how to play guitar yet... I realized that there is a way to hold on to something that doesn't exist yet. That's what takes place when a song is written: you see something that isn't there. Then you use your instrument to find it."

Perhaps this internal mechanism for songwriting is the gift that leads Flea to call him "the greatest musician in the world" and Kiedis—with more restraint and more vision—to observe "The artistic center of his brain is pretty much all of his brain."

For those who are wondering if any of this behavior was due to drug use, the answer is yes and no: "Around the time of *Blood Sugar Sex Magik*," he recalled, "Flea and I were smoking a lot of pot, especially me. Anthony wasn't, and it disconnected. I thought it was having a good effect on my music, which in a way it was. But it's the energy of the four of us that makes the music, not smoking pot or any other drug... I overestimated its influences. Writing has always come really naturally to me, but my recommendation to [a group of] musicians is that you all smoke pot or none of you do: it's good for a band to be together, be on the same plane. There's a lot less bad energies around now we're all coming from the same place." For many musicians and non-musicians, a quick hit on a joint isn't particularly good or bad for their creativity—but in the Chilis' case (and in particular the axis of Flea and Frusciante, the songwriting core) too much of it had disassociated them from the rest of the band—the currently clean Kiedis, who had his own demons to combat by staying drug-free, and drummer Smith, a defiantly blue-collar rocker who enjoys a beer but seems not to indulge in other substances more than infrequently.

How did John regard the first album he had cut as a Chili Pepper—the much more aggressive and complex *Mother's Milk*? Years later, he recalled, "That was our main 'macho' album. I don't really get into that emotion. I remember when I joined the band I had a very limited idea of what they were trying to do, and I just tried to fit in with that. But in time I started learning more about what kind of music they liked or what kind of ideas they were open to. Like when I first saw Flea wearing a Talking Heads T-shirt, I said, cool, he's into that too. And I started to realize we could do something with a much broader scope than what they had been doing."

In that case, how did he look back on his work on *Blood Sugar Sex Magik*, then, which most listeners would describe as nothing less than inspired? "On *Blood Sugar*... I was capable of playing much more than I did," he mused. "Not that I think it's bad guitar playing... But I was so concerned with doing everything in one take, I didn't really take any chances in the studio. With a couple of exceptions, I knew exactly what I was going to do. I think at that time I'm just completely improvising, and every solo has a real spontaneous, even haphazard feel to it. I'm not putting down my guitar playing: I just feel like I was capable of a whole lot of things instead of just cramming in every bit of technique that I possibly could... I'd rather hear someone play the best they're capable of with the minimum amount of technique, than someone with a lot of technique who plays without feeling."

He added, "To me, the real world and the various interactions we have with other human beings and things like that—that's not really...for me, that's not the core of what life is about. For me, the really important things about life are what takes place inside of people... the things that have nothing to do with the course of time or anything like that, but the things that take place within. That's what I'm interested in hearing in music and that's what I'm interested in in terms of my writing. I do like a personal song now and then—I'm definitely a sucker for songs about love and things like that. Sometimes I wish that I could feel totally comfortable with writing songs about love, like the doo-wop songs of the 1950s or something. I definitely love that kind of music, and there's something about the simplicity of those kinds of lyrics that I love. And that's why I do, occasionally, write songs like that, but they just don't seem to make it onto my records because for that reason they just seem too personal."

Frusciante is clearly his own strongest critic, dismissing the lyrical, stripped-down guitar playing of *Blood Sugar Sex Magik* for being laid down with too much focus on technique—the refuge of the insecure player, and the exact opposite of the simple approach that Flea had concentrated on finding. With this in mind, it's little wonder that a meltdown approached—and perhaps little wonder that *BSSM* is so good: it's the temporary blaze of a flame that would burn brightly, but briefly....

Flea (bass)

Despite the inner grief and communication problems of Anthony Kiedis, and the whirlwind of paranoia that was evolving in John Frusciante, Michael "Flea" Balzary looked back on the music of *Blood Sugar Sex Magik* with a deep appreciation as the years passed. "To me," he remarked, "*Blood Sugar* is the first time that we got down on tape what we really do. We'd never done that before. In the past, we'd always been intimidated by the studio. It would be a tense and alien environment. But that album was more about creating a vibe for us to jam and do our thing in."

Flea's childhood had been as bizarre as that of Kiedis, but with the unfortunate added elements of drug and alcohol abuse in his family, which made life all the tougher. "I was raised in a very violent, alcoholic household," said the Australian-born musician. "I grew up being terrified of my parents, particularly my father figures. My dad left when I was six, I didn't see him much, and my stepfather was aggressive. It caused a lot of trouble in later life." This grim situation led to the inevitable drug experimentation: "We did drugs from a very young age and it just started to kind of... steamroll," he said, adding, "Also, taking acid was a big thing for me as a youngster. I don't recommend drugs to anyone, but I can't deny that I did them. " The young Balzary hung out on LA street corners from the age of 11, sometimes not returning home until 4am. However, a fortuitous meeting changed his life, as he recalled. "Meeting Anthony Kiedis in high school had a lot to do with how I ended up as a musician. He was the first kid I met who didn't give a shit about being like anybody else. The way he talked, the way he dressed, and the way he acted had a big influence on me. He was so anti; he thought anyone who tried to be like anyone else was lame."

Flea was much more aggressive as a young man, and more eager to impress. He once told an interviewer who had asked if the Chilis were merely the hyped-up response to the public's desire for a white funk band that: "They can suck the juice out of my butthole, man—we're the granddaddy groove gooses, and we drink our smooth juices, and we're the slidenest, glidenest, movinest, groovinest, hippinest, hoppinest, rockinest, jamminest, slamminest... We're on a mission... We're on a mission to spread the cosmic love vibe and the rhythm of life and rock soulfully. We're for real... Sometimes they make a gimmick out of it. 'Hey! White guys working with a black guy, playing funk!' We play what we play because that's what we like, and we work with George [Clinton] because he's great. That's all there is to it."

The Clinton experience had been profound, he told the *NME* in 1985. "The only click track we had was George clapping, stamping and dancing around us. And when he was in the control room, he'd scream into the mic, 'Yeah, kick it! Do it! Get deep! Throw it down!' When George is doing that in your ear while you're playing you just go, whooooo whooooheeeooh! That's great. George is really spiritual like that, which is why he's 43 and still blowing it out... George was a fifth member of the band when we recorded the album, no doubt about it, but he didn't do anything we wouldn't have done completely on our own. He made it easy for us to do a lot of things, because he had access to the James Brown horn section, and he understood us but, if we'd had our way, the first album would have sounded like this too."

When the various bands that he and Kiedis co-founded gradually came together, Flea's love of music became his life's guiding principle. "Anthony and I would sit and listen to Eric Dolphy play 'God Bless The Child' on the bass clarinet over and over again, for about five hours. How could I not be deeply affected by that? I couldn't believe a human being was making that noise! There's nothing more amazing than a human creating that energy through an instrument. I've never reached that level, because I'm just not studied enough in music to do something as amazing as Eric Dolphy did."

Flea then took his love of jazz a stage further by taking up the trumpet, an instrument that he mastered to a certain degree (enough to play it on *Blood Sugar Sex Magik* and other, later recordings, notably 2004's *Live In Hyde Park*), but without becoming a jazz-theory expert. "I started playing trumpet when I was 11 years old," he said. "I've never played trumpet with the Chili Peppers. I did play a little with a [school] band called Thelonious Monster. It was always my dream to be a great jazz trumpet player. It still is."

In fact, even in his forties he still evidenced a desire to sharpen up his theory. As he explained, "A friend of mine, a great upright bassist named Hilliard Green, was talking to me about theory. The way he explains it, there are certain things very easily within my grasp; I just need to spend some time to figure them out. My music is based mostly on intuition and instinct, but I could go further with a better understanding of theory... I'd love to walk into a room and be able to play with [saxophonist] Wayne Shorter and [pianist] McCoy Tyner—that would be beautiful. I feel I could play well in any rock, reggae, funk, or African band in the world, but jazz... that's intense! I feel jazz, but I just don't know enough about theory to play it."

But it was the early LA punk wars that affected Flea most, allowing him to channel the emotions caused by his difficult circumstances into music. "Punk rock changed my life," he said. "As for punk rock music, though, I don't think it exists any more. I like Green Day, but they're more like an oldies pop band. Punk rock music ended with the Germs, but punk rock as an attitude hasn't. That means spitting in the face of convention and doing your own thing that's anti the bloated, corporate, boring, heard-it-a-billion-times-before bullshit. The bands that did it well were playing some of the most innovative, exciting music of their time—but now, it's about playing fun music and having a good time. That's cool, but it's not punk."

Flea later summed up his influences when he talked about his choice of listening material on tour: "We have like six tapes we've been listening to... Miles Davis's *Porgy And Bess*, a Muddy Waters compilation, a Velvet Underground, Black Flag's *Damaged*, an Echo & The Bunnymen, and one I can't remember. Miles Davis is just unbelievable. You listen to *Kind Of Blue*, and you hear all you'll ever have to. That was one of the first records I ever bought. I wore it out and replaced it."

Flea's life improved exponentially once punk and jazz had taken up their rightful places in his psyche and another crucial contact had been made—this time with Slovak, who had encouraged him to take up the bass guitar: "Hillel really [shook me up]. He got me to play the bass when we were in high school together. We had some incredible jams—we were the only two people in the world who could share that. It will never happen again... I remember the tone and texture of those conversations and they sometimes still inhabit me when I play. That's when I let things be natural."

Flea's relationship with Kiedis remained strong, and has endured solidly, despite the occasional argument. As Anthony explained: "We've been known to have our differences of opinion. But I don't think that's unusual. Any time two people know each other and work together and play together for as long as Flea and I have, the occasional disagreement is just an accepted part of the pie. We've been through so much together that if something were going to come between us, I think it would have happened years ago."

Although life was still weird for the kid from a broken home and insalubrious circumstances, the Hollywood existence suited the young Balzary. "Living in Hollywood, we've dealt with a lot of underground shit, hanging out with the local weirdos," explained Flea later. "At the same time, we were into driving out to the beach, going backpacking in the Sierras. We were into both things. And we couldn't have gotten that living anywhere but Hollywood."

In due course things got better still and Flea got married, shortly afterwards becoming a father to a daughter, Clara, who was born in September 1988. But he was about to be dealt the same bad card as Kiedis—and was laid out by the death of Slovak. He recalled, bitterly: "When Hillel died it was during one of the happiest times of my life. I was married and completely in love and had a baby on the way. I was smoking weed and playing basketball and going home and loving my wife. I felt very connected with a lot of people, but a lot of that was shattered. When Hillel died, I completely hit the deck." This was not helped by his subsequent divorce from Clara's mother, Loesha.

Luckily, Flea's band needed him more than ever and with the recruitment of John Frusciante—who would be a spiritual companion almost as much as Slovak had been—he soldiered on, veering into drug abuse but never allowing himself to be swallowed up by it. At 31, after the enormous success of *Blood Sugar Sex Magik* and the subsequent bout of touring that finished Frusciante and almost did the same for him, he hit the bottom. "I was this incredible burst of wildness, and suddenly I was hacked down… I got sick. I had chronic fatigue for a year. My system completely collapsed. But I was forced to confront things about myself."

Also like the guitarist, one of the problems that Flea experienced in the wake of *BSSM* was that the Chilis' rise to rock star level felt both inappropriate and incongruous. "It's something other people see you as, and you have to take it with a grain of salt," said Flea, adding that from time to time he would react intolerantly to over-zealous fans—and then feel "terribly disgusted and apologetic afterwards."

And yet he had to continue. In the end, after months of trauma, he found himself once again as a bandmember. "My position goes beyond that of just a bass player; I also consider myself an entertainer. As a bassist, my job is to kick ass. When I pick up my bass and play with the band, it's time to get serious. It's my job to give my all every time I play, no matter how I feel. But I also buy into the showbiz aesthetic of giving a dazzling performance, and I'm into putting on a show," he explained

His rather more serious role as a father helped to ground him. "Being a dad is definitely part of [recovery]. It also comes from becoming a more aware person," he pondered. "I was stoned every day of my life for 15 years, which I don't regret. I've done a lot of shitty things to myself, but everything's for a reason—so if I can be more aware of what's going on around me, then I'm going to be a better person and a better musician. Now, I meditate every day. It means so much to sit and be quiet. I just feel what's going on inside myself, and it's helped me to be more in touch with my feelings—with my purest level of expression. It also helps me to remove the blocks between my heart and my brain so I'm able to express myself and not be worried about some stupid bullshit."

Flea is the heart of the Red Hot Chili Peppers and at the heart of every album they have made—especially *Blood Sugar*

Sex Magik, with its huge, unforgettable bass parts. He should take much of the credit for it, and for books, such as this one, that celebrate it.

Chad Smith (drums)

"Unspoken musical telepathy," is how Detroit-born Chad Smith, the most jovial, solid, and in many ways the most uncomplicated Chili Pepper, describes the remarkable unspoken relationship between the bandmembers. He's the epitome of the drummer cliché—manly, dependable and not given to tortured self-analysis (although he did refuse to sleep in the haunted house during the *Blood Sugar Sex Magik* sessions, preferring to ride his Harley home every night).

While Frusciante is a man guided by inner voices, Flea is a tortured aesthete, and Kiedis can be a boy in a man's body at times, Chad tends to enjoy life without much difficulty. However, he did tell one interviewer—who had quizzed him about the fact that he has three children with three different mothers—"I'm the dumper. I fall in love easily, but... I get restless. I'll figure it out one day. Can we talk about something else?"

Politically, he can be outspoken at times, once saying: "I'd like to meet George Bush [Sr.] and tell him what a great job I think he's doing with the country and that I'm gonna vote for him as long as he wants to say in office, He's doing such a great job with the whole thing—education, drugs, the economy, and America in general. So I'd like to compliment him on that. But in all seriousness..."

"Michigan, smoking pot and drinking, occasionally too much," was how Smith summed up his youth, adding: "I started playing when I was a wee lad, when I was seven. I have an older brother named Brad—he's a guitarist, and my sister played piano. This was in the early 1970s, so I don't know if I had an affinity for hitting things or not, but I started out on Baskin-Robbins ice-cream cartons, and Lincoln Logs building-blocks for sticks. I eventually trashed those and then my parents thought I would stick with it—so I got one of those starter pads that comes with those snare drum starter kits." His first musical influences were appropriate for a future Chili Pepper: "Black Sabbath, Led Zeppelin, Cream, The Doors, George Clinton and Parliament-Funkadelic, and of course, The Jimi Hendrix Experience. Flea and Anthony are into funk, like old-school Meters and stuff like that. Flea got into rock later on in life, came up in jazz as a jazz trumpet player, and then got into punk rock, playing in Fear and stuff like that. All of us come from different backgrounds as far as musical influences come from."

Asked about his influences, he mused, "There's just so many. Shit, man. Drummer-wise would help me to narrow it down. Gene Krupa, bringing the drums into the fore, not just being a guy sitting in the dark, had a lot to do with changing the way people perceive drums and the way that drummers are involved with bands. So I'd say mostly the dead guys. When I die, hopefully I'll join them in percussion heaven!"

After private tuition failed to make an impact, Smith honed his chops by playing along with the greats. "I took a private lesson, but it didn't really work out, so I went back to playing along with records," he said. "That's really the thing that got me into playing a lot—getting excited about playing along with my favorite bands like Zeppelin and Black

Sabbath. And then I played in public school. I was in every band class I could get in, like after-school jazz band and marching band, and that's where I really learned to read music, from elementary all the way through junior high and high school." A professional musical lifestyle soon followed, even including a record deal: "I played in a band called Rockin' Conspiracy, with my older brother. Our hit tune was was called 'Whiplash'," he sniggered. "Maybe I could get the Chili Peppers to cover that... My older brother Brad had his S&H Greenstamps guitar with his strings about three feet off the neck. He was such a big influence on me, and being a couple of years older than me, he had all the cool records. Then he went to college and I went right into music and started playing professionally out of high school. I just played with everyone, playing bars and clubs. I played with people who were better than me and it made me improve; played most places in Detroit. I joined a band called Toby Red in Detroit in 1984—we had a record on RCA that came and went pretty quick."

Detroit lost its appeal after Smith's tenure in Toby Red, so he upped sticks and moved to Los Angeles, where he intended to study at college. "I had sort of exhausted all the avenues playing in Detroit," he recalled, "so again, through the stewardship of my brother, I ended up in California and went to the Musicians' Institute in LA. I wanted to get better as a player. I met the guys through a friend of a friend, and their former drummer [Jack Irons] had quit. I wasn't too familiar with the Chili Peppers before that, so I joined at the end of 1988 and we finished recording *Mother's Milk* at the end of 1989. Next thing I know I'm in *Spin* magazine with a sock on my dick..."

Career progression, indeed... the band soon honed a songwriting method that was as spontaneous as it was dextrous, and led to the raw feel that made *Blood Sugar Sex Magik* so gripping. As Chad put it, "We always feel pretty creative as far as writing songs [goes]. We write them together; we just get in a room, or on occasion in Flea's garage. We just sort of improvise, like jazz musicians. It's very sort of spontaneous and organic, not a preconceived sort of jamming. Now we record everything, because sometimes you'll forget, you know, 'what was that thing again?' So we record everything. Sometimes one of us will have a riff or a bass-line from home, but it really gels when we come together. We really have a strong special chemistry that we take advantage of when we get together."

Smith recalled the *Blood Sugar Sex Magik* sessions with fondness, but with a realistic take on the band's relatively fragile frame of mind during the sessions. "John was going through a really rough time," he pondered. "He was very miserable and he was acting a little crazy... He was put on this earth to play music with us, and I certainly think that he's come into the realization that being in a rock band is not a bad thing. It's not evil, it can be one of the most beautiful experiences anyone can have, so I'm not worried about John at all... I don't think you have to be a tortured soul to play great music, and I think sometimes some of the best music comes when you're just happy." Of the maverick guitarist, he concluded: "He's the most unique guy I've ever known. Outside of having an incredible, natural talent, he's just immensely focused and disciplined and plays so much and cares so much. He's widely knowledgeable about the huge expansive quantity of music and the history of music. He has a lot to refer to, he has great taste, he's really smart. And he can play the guitar like a motherfucker, and he doesn't sound like anyone else when he plays it."

Affable to the end, Smith is even happy to recommend equipment and playing tips to those who seek his advice, explaining the method which led him to *Blood Sugar Sex Magik*: "Playing along with records is key. Playing well with others is important—not being too flashy, just keeping good time and of course coming up with cool beats. And as far as equipment goes, it has gotten so much more affordable and the drum sets are of great quality. I play Pearl; their Export Series is great for a beginner. Go to a store or any kind of music store and you can get a good kit for a good price. You don't need much, just a four- or five-piece kit. It also depends on what kind of music you're playing; with rock music you just need something pretty basic... I'm certainly no expert. Drums all have their own particulars—each drum has a place where they sound the best—where they ring out and resonate the best, and the head surface isn't too loose or too tight, mainly so you get a good rebound off the head. There are obviously all kinds of drum/head combinations—like if you're playing jazz music you want thinner heads—but if you're playing rock music you want something thicker because you're hitting them harder."

A master of the jazz, funk and rock idioms, Smith was bang on target when he pointed out that "playing well with others is important—not being too flashy, just keeping good time and of course coming up with cool beats" was the key thing in jamming with a band. The telepathy he had referred to came about because of precisely this—the ability to hear or even feel the music coming from another person on a real, profoundly emotional level—and it's this that makes his contribution to *Blood Sugar Sex Magik* so memorable.

Rick Rubin (producer)

Over the five decades of rock music, it's become a relatively common cliché that the producer of a given band is referred to gushingly as the fourth, fifth, sixth or so on member of that band, thanks to the influence he or she wields to make the music what it is. Look at the 'fifth Beatle' George Martin, for example—or closer to home, fader-tweaker Ross Robinson, whose work on Korn's debut album of 1994 was so integral to the record that the band included him as a member in the CD booklet.

But in the case of *Blood Sugar Sex Magik*, it's not going too far to label producer Rick Rubin as the fifth Chili Pepper. So far reaching was his understanding of the music the band were trying to produce, how best to make that process a success and how to manage the band while doing so, that his presence is stamped all over the album—just as it is over the other key albums in his production *oeuvre*, The Beastie Boys' *License To Ill*, Slayer's *Reign In Blood*, The Cult's *Electric*, and System Of A Down's self-titled and *Toxicity* albums. The dry, deep sound that he brings to a record, with musically rhetorical elements stripped away and the strengths of the musicians brought to the fore, is his trademark—and one that is all over *Blood Sugar Sex Magik*.

As he explained, Rubin had been interested in the idea of working with the Chilis for some time before he actually agreed to do so. "I was involved with college radio and was way into the Red Hot Chili Peppers before *Blood Sugar Sex Magik*, and especially was a huge fan of Flea. I was also one of the few guys at the radio station that knew he was a trumpet player and into jazz. Their love and appreciation of music, and the musicianship between the players in that band, the level of interactivity in their playing—I don't think there are any other big bands that do that, that really jam. They really do. They can play anything, and they listen to each other, which is so rare." He added: "[In] a lot of bands, people just play their parts, but the Chili Peppers are truly an interactive band, kind of in the way that musicians might have been in the 1960s. That's one of the reasons that there were so many bands back then; it was a different kind of musicianship. It was about playing together, playing off each other, complementing each other. Really, John Frusciante and Flea have this kind of magical interaction, almost like a psychic relationship."

The raw strength of the Flea/Frusciante axis was something that Rubin spotted early in his working relationship with the Chilis—and not surprisingly so, given his ability to identify key players within whatever musical act he was involved. As he said of Public Enemy, whom he had championed from the early days: "Chuck D changed the whole world of rap. When everyone was just bragging or dissing, he had serious social commentary and talked about serious things when nobody else was. I can remember when [Public Enemy debut album] *Yo! Bum Rush The Show* came out. Radio stations would only play the instrumental versions, because they liked the tracks but hated Chuck's voice. And then on *It Takes a Nation of Millions To Hold Us Back* he said, 'Last time you played the music, this time you'll play the lyrics.' That's what he was talking about."

The areas of Rubin's experience and character that made him so perfect for the Chilis production role—hip-hop, heavy metal, the handling of politically sensitive music, learning how to survive the record industry—are not common to any other producer, making him the ideal man for the job. All this talent and awareness needed a pretty spacious ego to fit into, of course, with Rubin pointing out to one interviewer who had quizzed him about his reputation as a difficult man to work with, that "I always listen to what other people have to say. Sometimes they're right and I learn something." It required material of unusual or significant nature to move him, he explained: "I like extreme things— good, bad. I like it when people take things to their limits, regardless of whether or not I agree. Because I think that's the only way we find out about new things... I'm bored by regular stuff. Things really excite me or else they mean nothing to me. I don't like anything that's mediocre. I'd never talk about anything [with the words] 'Oh, that was OK.' I hate it or I love it." As for that supposedly difficult reputation, he shrugged: "I need to be in control. And I'm a good boss. I mean, I'm an effective leader in terms of getting people to get things done. I can motivate people to do good work. People take what I say seriously, which is good."

Rubin's early career with the Def Jam record label, which had been so crucial to the development of East Coast hip-hop, had been executed on the strength of his instincts, he explained. "We just tried to make music that we loved, for ourselves. One of the reasons that [the Beastie Boys'] *License To Ill* was as diverse as it was, is that we really did it over a long period of time. We probably recorded it over two years, really slowly, writing a song and then writing another song six weeks or two months later. By taking so long, it really gave it a breadth and depth that's difficult from a typical album where an artist has six weeks to write their songs for a record."

It's interesting to note that the Chilis and the Beastie Boys were often compared at one point in their careers—a comparison that irked the former no end. "That comparison," said Kiedis with gritted teeth, "is made from a standpoint of ignorance. If you look at both bands you'll see immediately that one is a band and one isn't. We create live, organic, fresh, in-your-face music every night. They go onstage and lip-synch to a turntable. Enjoying their records is one thing, but live they're one of the most boring bands you could ever waste your money on. If you see our name and theirs in the same line, it's because we're both white."

"Anthony raps all the time," Flea added, "and it's a beautiful thing, but no way are we a rap band. Rap today is completely associated with drum machines and synthesizers, which is not the deal with us. We're not hip-hop, we're a hardcore psychedelic funk band."

The rapping of Rubin's earlier signings, which Anthony Kiedis would emulate to perfection on *Blood Sugar Sex Magik* and earlier Chilis records, was nurtured by Def Jam with much effort—at little reward—by Rubin and his then-business partner Russell Simmons: "I was going to New York University and I was into rap music at the time, but there weren't a lot of rap records coming out; and the rap records that were coming out weren't representative of what the rap scene really was," mused the producer. "I used to go to the rap clubs in New York—I'd be the only white guy there—and they'd be playing rock 'n' roll records with guys rapping over them. Like [Aerosmith's] "Walk This Way", [which] was an original record that every rap DJ would have and use. Billy Squier's 'Big Beat' was another one. And the rap records that were coming out at the time were like Sugar Hill records, which were essentially disco records with people rapping over them. Kids who liked rap bought them because there weren't any records representative of their rap scene. So, I saw this void and starting making those records, just because I was a fan and wanted them to exist." And so, thanks to this middle-class white guy's instincts, the biggest movement in black music in the last decade of the century was given a head-start...

And yet it was all such a grass-roots operation, as Rubin explained: "The way it started was... the first record I made, I was planning on putting it out myself strictly for the purpose of breaking even—making back my costs, that was always the plan—and I sold it to Streetwise Records, who offered me more than I thought I was going to make if I'd sold as many as I wanted to. Then, as it turned out, it was a hit; it sold, I don't know, 100,000 12-inches in the New York area, which was a big deal."

The fact that Rubin brought his white rock influences to the music was crucial, making hip-hop a highly appealing force for white as well as black music fans and sparking off a chain of progression which led directly to *Blood Sugar Sex*

Magik: "My high school was, like, 70 percent white, 30 percent black. The kids in my high school liked Led Zeppelin, Pink Floyd... One of the contributions I think I had to rap was the song structure. Before I started, a lot of rap records were like a verse from beginning to end—just three guys trading off vocals, starting at the beginning and finishing when they finished, maybe six minutes later."

"I tried to make rap into songs," he added later, "which is now the way they are. I think I helped bring it to the masses. The fact that the Beastie Boys were a white group was kind of a big deal. If a 14-year-old white girl in, oh, Alabama had brought home a Run-DMC album in those days—you know, looking at these black guys as rock 'n' roll guys or sex symbols—it would not really have been OK. Whereas, as stupid and disgusting as the Beastie Boys might have been, that was OK because they were white. Reality is, this is a very racist country, *very* racist. I think when they played the Beastie Boys on MTV, then it made it easier for MTV to play Run-DMC."

The axis of influence worked both ways, with the black crowd's vociferous love of their music much more palatable to the young Rubin than the slacker, laid-back white audiences of the 1970s. "I didn't like what the [white rock] crowd was doing... It wasn't a real thing. And then, all the black kids liked rap records, and one week their favorite would be one group and then a new single would come out and they would have a new favorite group. It was that immediate. It was a very immediate, progressive audience. It was very exciting, and you could be part of it. You could go and hear it and see it and feel it and touch it."

"It felt like outsider music to begin with," he explained of the first hip-hop records. "It was completely underground, and just happened to be made by black people. I felt like when I was submerged in it, I was as well-versed in it as anyone else. I felt like the music made a kinship that transcended skin color. Everyone was a fan. It was a shared passion... My favorite group at the time was Treacherous Three, and I met with one of the guys in the band... There were no stars in rap music. It was really just a work of passion. Everyone who was doing it was doing it because they loved it, not because anyone thought it was a career."

His expectations were about to be confounded. Over the next five years, Def Jam became an institution, despite the inexperience of Rubin and Simmons. "We didn't even think about having a hit single. We just tried to do something we liked. There were no expectations whatsoever. The only hope was that we'd sell enough records to make enough money to make another record. If it didn't cost us money to have Def Jam, we'd be happy. If it supported itself, and we could keep doing it, we'd be doing it," he explained.

By the time Rick came to work with the Chilis, he had learned a few things about the industry since those early days, when: "I didn't know anything about the record business, but I recognized that the hip-hop records that were coming out that I would buy as a fan, and the music I would hear when I'd go to the club, were two different things".

"The music in the club was much more breakbeat, scratching, raw, kind of rock-based," he added. "The hip-hop records that were coming out at the time were really like disco or R&B, but with a person rapping on it instead of a girl singing on it. I guess what I set out to do as a fan was to make records that sounded like what I liked about going to a hip-hop club, and trying to document that scene."

Like that of the Chilis, Rubin's career has hinged upon fortuitous meetings with the right people—in his case, Russell Simmons. "We met at a party," he recalled. "I had produced a record called 'It's Yours' by T La Rock and Jazzy Jay. That was a pretty big club record in New York City. It was played on the radio, too, but it was a New York-area local hit. I met Russell a few months after that came out, and he said it was his favorite record, and he was so excited to meet me, and couldn't believe that I was white. There was nobody white doing anything in hip-hop, and here was his favorite hip-hop record made by a white guy. I was really excited to meet him, because his name was on all these great records, like Kurtis Blow. He was already a mogul of rap music, even though there was no business. It was just a small, underground scene. He was already kind of the focal point."

Both men also knew that success in these circles didn't necessarily mean the financial kind: "I never got paid," laughed Rubin. "And I learned how the independent record business works; I still haven't been paid to this date... Russell [had] made about 20 hit records that sold a lot, and he was broke. He never got paid either. So I said, 'This is dumb. They're not really doing much for us, and they're not paying us, so let's do it ourselves. At least we can make sure we get paid and our artists get paid'... It just turns out, I was really making records before I became a record company; I was producing records first. The record company became a function of the production. In other words, I knew we could get paid, whereas I didn't know we could get paid when I was delivering records to other people. And it damages your relationship with your artists when they don't get paid—it's your fault. So, I tried to do away with as many of the problems... Instead of going to somebody and asking them to do the things that needed to get done, and not getting them done, it was easier to just take on the responsibility. It was just not going to get done unless I did it."

Once Def Jam was up and running, Rubin learned about finances. "Rap records can be made very inexpensively... the first LL Cool J album—the whole album—cost $7,000 to record and we sold 900,000 copies when we first came out. We were already selling to CBS at that time, so that's where that much came from." He also learned the importance of instinctive operation. "Really, the key to it is doing what you believe in, as opposed to what you think is going to work. There were never any plans to make anything happen. I just did what I liked and believed in it, and luckily it all worked out. You just have to do what you want to do and be good at what you do. Be good at your craft. I do what I like, and I believe what I like will work. I don't put barriers up."

This no-barriers approach served Rubin well when he came to work on *Blood Sugar Sex Magik*, notably on enormous successes such as "Under The Bridge" (which he advised the initially reluctant singer Kiedis to record) and "Give It Away", on which he advised Flea to keep the instantly memorable bass part (the song's obvious hook after the singer's delivery of the title line) simple and elegant.

This methodology stemmed from the raw, home-made operations of the early Def Jam, as he recalled: "[Hip-hop] wasn't slick, and it wasn't mainstream, but it was alternative, edgy, raw music. There's a homemade and handmade quality to it. Like if you listen to Sugar Hill albums, or the hip-hop records that came out on Enjoy and Tommy Boy, those are all of our competitors. They came before us, but became our competitors. Those records are all very different than ours."

Perfect groundwork, then, for *Blood Sugar Sex Magik*, whose simple, effective production was a world away in operational terms from contemporary competitors such as— for example—the same year's *Metallica* album, which had taken over a year to record. Even Simmons wasn't quite clued in to Rubin's instinctual approach at first, telling him of Public Enemy: "You're wasting your time. This is black punk rock. This is garbage. You could make pop records, why are you wasting your time on Public Enemy?" Rubin's response: "Because they're the greatest group in the world. Because the pop records are the ones that aren't important. *This* is what's important, you'll see."

By the time Rick entered the Laurel Canyon mansion with Kiedis et al, his record company was huge, but his approach to music had not changed a jot. "You know, artists come in all the time and ask us 'What are you looking for?' he said. "It doesn't matter what we're looking for. You do what you do, and if you do it well, people will like it. And if they don't like it, you should be pumping gas. That's just the way it is. It's either right or wrong, and if it's right, it will happen… I don't want to become an A&R guy who goes out seven nights a week searching for acts. I don't do that. But I keep aware, I read magazines and I just *feel* what's going on. I try to understand culture as much as music, because it really works together. You know, art has always reflected culture. It's never been the other way." Rubin knew how important he had been to hip-hop, of course, but acknowledged that the music rose above personal contributions such as his: "I recognize my role in it, but had I not been around... I think it would have gone a different route. But the strength of hip-hop is beyond any of the individuals involved. It really was a wave. We just happened to be in a good spot on the wave. The wave was coming."

The other side of the Rubin coin—the side that attracted the Chilis to him just as much as his love of black music drew him to them—was his hardcore punk and metal obsessions, making him the embodiment of the dual strands of music that informed the band. Again, it was the vibe and feel of the emotion in this music which had gripped Rubin.

"The first time I saw Slayer, I'd never heard of them," he said. "This was at the time they were playing so fast you couldn't even tell what they were playing, it was just a blur. But the command they had of the audience, I'd never seen anything like it. Something there I'd never heard of! They had such an arrogant presence on stage, and they had this sold-out place of kids killing themselves, into the music—jumping around, stage-diving, everything—the band so... arrogant and not caring. They knew. They *knew* that it was right. Do you know what I'm saying? They weren't smiling, it wasn't like that. It was a very serious... They did not care what was going on, because they knew that they were good. The audience respected it and were 100 percent with them."

Such intensity was, he reckoned, the future of heavy metal: "The Metallicas, the Slayers, the Anthraxes of this world are replacing the Judas Priests and the Iron Maidens. Those bands aren't exciting any more. I think the old guard once had this attitude, and as time went on the success thing struck, and they wanted to compete or outdo themselves instead of doing what they *felt* was right, or really reaching for new things. They weren't reaching to push boundaries, they were reaching to try to sell a few more records, make some more money."

But he was always aware of quality control ("Unfortunately, there are a lot of metal bands that aren't very good and that go through the motions and get popular, but it's a very short-term, meaningless kind of success") and the self-cannibalizing nature of even the best music. "With punk, I remember thinking at the time that it was odd that so many American punk bands were singing about this class struggle and political oppression, when we weren't really feeling that. They were imitating what the English bands were singing about. There's always some of that, taking from itself. Rappers talking about the same types of things: bragging and dissing are kinda the main themes on early hip-hop records."

However, Rubin always admired the effect that punk had had on the actual making of the music. "Punk rock took the music out of Madison Square Garden and brought it back to this kind of naïve street level where anyone could do it, even those who are not really musicians. Hip-hop did the same thing, where you didn't have to be Luther Vandross or Herbie Hancock. You could just be a guy with an idea. That was enough for you to make a record."

Rubin was—like Flea and Kiedis—also keenly aware of the nature, one might almost say the personality, of Los

Angeles. "We here in Los Angeles are really spoiled with all this good stuff, like rock 'n' roll and clubs, and there being a scene," he maintained. "It's nice, when you're doing any kind of art, to be able to see the effect. It helps you do it. It's just the fact that the community exists [that makes you feel] good, makes you want to do it.

"In New York, all it is is numbers on a page... it's nice to be able to make a record and turn on the radio so you can hear it, and go to a club... There's a scene revolving around this kind of music that doesn't exist in New York. In New York, it's like making records in a vacuum. You never hear your records on the radio, because radio is all Top 40, there's no rock 'n' roll station."

Another way in which Rubin was directly suited for the role of producer with the Red Hot Chili Peppers was that he possesses a keen awareness of the politics of music, and had strong opinions about censorship—something that the Chilis had confronted before and would do again.

"I think people should be allowed to sing about what they feel, whatever that is," he said. "It's about the extremes, and about people believing in what they believe in. If Public Enemy wants to do songs about killing whitey, and I'm whitey, that's fine; and I'll support them in that attempt, as long as what they do is good musically, which is all I really care about. It's only commentary. I don't think music can change the world. It's OK to say anything in art. Public Enemy are not politicians. All they do is try to entertain people. I don't think records can make people do anything. And I don't think there's anything people shouldn't be exposed to. I think people should be exposed to all the ideas that are out there. It's OK. If you don't like what's on TV, turn it off."

Asked where responsibility lay for exposure to challenging material for children, he replied squarely, "I think it's the parents' responsibility to teach kids values. TV, records, all these things are solely entertainment, for kids as well. The *only* responsibility an artist has to his audience is to entertain. And I don't care how they do it. Knowledge is always good—whether it's good or bad. Not letting people have information... Again, it's just all information. And everybody should have [access to] all information, and people can choose whether to like it or not, to agree with it or disagree with it. No one can make anybody do anything they don't believe. I think an upbringing is where people learn their values, and all artists can do is entertain people. Otherwise, when they get into politics, when they start preaching, their audience will leave them and they'll have no value at all, even as an entertainer... A kid who commits suicide doesn't do it because the lyrics tell him to—it just doesn't happen—unless he was going to do it anyway."

This basic approach underpinned all the music he was involved in, no matter what style or genre, as he explained. "I don't think I'm going to run the risk of getting stale, because I don't make the same record. If you listen to my records, they don't really sound the same. Unlike a Stock-Aitken-Waterman record where the artists are interchangeable, or Desmond Child—I think all of his records sound the same, whether it's Alice Cooper or Bon Jovi singing them, it's a Desmond Child song. I try not to fall into that trap because I think it's limiting, I think it's short-term... I think I've progressed a lot musically. I feel like, because I'm aware of the cultural things going on, and because I allow my tastes to change and not say, 'Oh, I sold millions of records making rap records, I have to keep making them,' I'm happy to say, 'Oh, well, I like speed metal this week, so I'm going to make speed metal records. And fuck it, I don't care if my speed metal records sell or don't, this is what I want to do.' Or, I may decide I want to make retro, 1960s-sounding records because that's what I like and that's what I'm going to do.'"

Rubin's split with Simmons and his launch of the new Def American label was key to the sequence of events that led him to the producer's chair in the Laurel Canyon studio. As he explained, "Russell and I were going in different directions, both musically and business-wise. And I thought that being as we were good friends, it would be better for us to break off and still be able to be friends, instead of some day hating each other—being in business together and it being a big, ugly mess. So, I said, 'Do you want to leave?' And he said, 'No,' and I said, 'OK, fine—I'll leave.' And we're still friends."

This allowed him to expand his horizons, as he said, "I believe in the validity of art. It's funny, because I'm against politics and I think musically that there's got to be a reason this is happening. Like treading new ground, like doing something that's not what's already on the radio. Rather than doing something that's already on the radio, so that's what we should do because then we'll get on the radio, too. That's not valid... There's never going to be a new Prince. There's Prince, and that's that. How many guys out here think they're the next Guns N' Roses? Guns N' Roses is Guns N' Roses. That's that."

The new label also meant that Rubin could meet unusual people—artists with unorthodox visions—and diversify his activities. "I probably am attracted to bizarre things. I'd like to call them progressive things," he mused. "If you look historically at the biggest bands in the world, they've always been progressive and new. I mean, even The Beatles were a punk rock band; you know, The Beatles used to play with toilet seats around their necks... A lot of times that mentality is needed to get up on stage and do what you have to do. Again, we're talking about those people with that special magic, the people who light up a dark room; you have to be prepared to take whatever comes along with it... I'm good with artists a lot of times whom a lot of people consider difficult, because I understand the way they think. I hate all the same shit they hate.

"Everything happens kind of the way it's supposed to happen, and we just watch it unfold," he shrugs, the perfect philosophical accompaniment to the Red Hot Chili Peppers' worldview. "And you can't control it. Looking back, you can't say, 'I should've...' You didn't, and had you, the outcome would have been different."

Brendan O'Brien (engineer)

Finally, *Blood Sugar Sex Magik* was engineered by Brendan O'Brien, who went on to become a much-respected producer in his own right, working with Korn, the Stone Temple Pilots and other alternative rock bands. The latter band's singer Scott Weiland (now of Velvet Revolver) once said of Brendan, "We have a really good chemistry [with him]... His input and energy are so wonderful that it makes it a joy to record. It is just a whole language between an artist and a producer. The artist is trying to get across what it is you want it to sound like on tape. It is really impossible to explain what it is you are trying to get on tape, so it is the job of the producer to interpret that language and get it on tape the way the artist wants to hear it. Brendan has always had a wonderful and natural ability to do that. You don't even have to say what you are going for, and sometimes it comes out better than you ever expected... and, on top of him being a great guy, he is really, really fast, which is how we like to work... by the time you get done explaining it he has it patched in and done."

In the next decade O'Brien would extend his producing palette to work with rock acts such as the British band The Music, whose singer Rob Harvey described the experience of working with him as "Really eye-opening. He's one of the only geniuses I've met in my life. He's a naturally gifted musician. He can just pick a guitar up and just show you something that he's never worked out before or anything. He can just play it instantly. He has a great vision as well. He just turned out all these new ideas... structuring songs, about keys, about how to record instruments, how to have a decent team around you to keep a studio running properly. A lot of studios are pretty much just a shambles. It's people hanging around saying, 'Let's do this now.' 'All right, yeah.' He was almost military, kind of—just constantly working, pulling different songs, doing a couple of songs a day. Mixing took him a couple of days, which usually takes a couple of weeks."

The work O'Brien performed on *Blood Sugar Sex Magik* is subtle but crucial. As engineer working under the eyes of the formidable Rubin, his role would have been to ensure that the raw quality of the recordings he captured—for Rubin then to manipulate and place in the songs—was of the maximum quality possible. While this is manageable enough in a professional studio with banks of permanent equipment and scientifically engineered acoustics, in the Laurel Canyon haunted house, making sure that microphones and amplifiers produced and received the full range of sounds and functioned at optimum levels would have presented a serious challenge.

But the fruits of O'Brien's labors are there for all to hear. All the instruments on the album sound fresh, clear, and warm, with immense presence and clarity, without ever sounding over-digitized or over-processed—the trap of so many modern recordings. This would have been aided by the vintage recording equipment and instruments the band used, of course, and their tremendous musical skill—but if the Chilis' mission had been to strip down their sound to the basic minimum to ensure musical honesty, the fact that they were so successful is at least partly down to O'Brien.

the songs

The magic in the grooves

"The album title is an eloquent but abstract description of how we feel," says Kiedis. "We live in a world packed with desensitizing forces that strip the world of magic. And music can help restore a sense of magic. The world is full of negativity, but we fight back with positivity. We're inspired by oceans, forests, animals, Marx Brothers films. We can't help but project uplifting vibrations, because we love each other so much and get off on playing together."

With these pithy words, the singer, speaking to *The Observer* in September 1991, summed up—with admirable honesty but significant hubris—the ethos that had filled the Chilis' working methods since the new line-up had first come together. Suffering from the death of Slovak but invigorated by the talents of Smith and Frusciante, the band was now in a position to work on exorcizing its demons and rise to a new level of psychological development. The results were musically and lyrically astounding.

The Power Of Equality
Blood Sugar Sex Magik opens with a sly move. When the album was released and the band made much in press interviews of their new, simpler, more economical musical approach, listeners were initially dumbfounded by the first track, "The Power Of Equality"—four minutes of hot-buttered funk that

could have been lifted from a *Mother's Milk* session, slap-and-pop bassline, meathead descending riff, and all. That's not to say it isn't a song to treasure: the nifty central duet between Flea and Frusciante is a beauty to hear, as are Smith's tightly nailed drums—with a big sound courtesy of the unusual recording environment—and Kiedis's mastery of a melodic vocal. No longer just a rapper with occasional forays into actual singing, Kiedis demonstrates from the off that he can cover all the required bases.

Lyrically, Anthony is pissed off. "American equality has always been sour," he sneers, adding "Red, black or white / This is my fight." He's musing on the state of racial equality in the USA, it's clear, promising "Death to the message / Of the Ku Klux Klan," referring to "Blackest anger" / "Whitest fear", and concluding, "Whatever happened to humanity?" This degree of social commentary had been heard before on Chili Peppers albums, but rarely with such controlled venom and certainly not accompanied by as effective a barrage of images.

Perhaps the best way to analyze Kiedis's decision to open the album with an anti-racism call to arms is to bear in mind the context of the day. As LA residents and most other Californians will recall, at the time that Kiedis composed these words, Los Angeles was a mere year or so away from the worst riots of its history. The issue of urban conflict between the city's black and Korean communities and the LA police department was in the news—which is not to say that the problem had not existed before, nor that it does not continue to exist today. This is simply a note that the issue was one to which the media were paying a high degree of attention at the time.

The run-up to the greatest act of riotous destruction in American history is not explained easily: too many factors contributed to the riots that levelled sections of Los Angeles for the six days following April 29, 1992 for any brief explanation to be accurate. However, consider vice president Dan Quayle's Commonwealth Club speech after the riots. He said, "When I have been asked during these last weeks who caused the riots and the killing in LA, my answer has been direct and simple. Who is to blame for the riots? The rioters are to blame. Who is to blame for the killings? The killers are to blame."

Ten years later, it seems to many who remember the disturbances that it was primarily the police beating of Rodney King that caused them—but in retrospect, his involvement was merely the last in a long line of incidents, each of which raised the temperature of inner-city LA (and most prominently in poorer areas such as South Central) until the anger felt by many of the city's oppressed residents reached breaking point. Kiedis, in his angry lyrics, was merely reflecting this tension.

More serious indications of the state of the nation—which had endured a decade of Republican policies—could be seen in the decay of the city ghettos, a direct result of the deprioritization of the urban poor by the federal government under Reagan and then George Bush Sr. Although the global recession that had plagued so much economic growth in those dark years had affected everyone, not just the residents of the run-down city districts, its impact on suburbs such as Compton had led to a measurable increase in crime and a quantifiable rise in poverty. Couple this with the often over-zealous reaction of the police to the increased urban crime levels in these areas, and all the explosive atmosphere required was a spark to ignite it. In this case, the spark was Rodney King—but the broader picture is that years of reduced domestic spending had prepared the ground for the rioters. And the looting that took place? Simply the instincts of a generation educated in Reaganomics: the children of Republicanism had come home to roost at last, it seems.

The *Washington Times* journalist Lou Cannon wrote an excellent book about those days of spring madness entitled *Official Negligence: How Rodney King And The Riots Changed Los Angeles And The LAPD*, in which he analyzed the roots of the conflict and the riots themselves. In it he revealed that the LAPD was riddled with institutional dysfunction, embracing racial bias wholeheartedly and applying those principles to the execution of their work. When Public Enemy said: "911 Is A Joke", it seems that they knew what they were talking about, as did Kiedis with "The Power Of Equality".

It's little wonder that the Chilis perceived racial tension at the time. On March 16, a Korean grocer, Soon Ja Du, had accused a 15-year-old girl, Latasha Harlins, of trying to steal a $1.79 bottle of orange juice. A security camera in the store showed Harlins slapping Du repeatedly, Du throwing a stool at her, and then, after Harlins had turned to walk away, Du raising a pistol and shooting her in the back. She was found guilty of voluntary manslaughter and the Compton Superior Court judge sentenced the shopkeeper to five years' probation, 400 hours of community service and a fine of $500. This came as a shock to many—the initial expectation was that Du would get an 11-year jail sentence. This caused protests among LA's

African-American communities, and the fact that many Korean businesses were attacked during the riots (in fact, 75 percent of the businesses attacked were Korean-run) can be directly attributed to the bad blood between the blacks and the Koreans that had arisen from this single case.

And then there was the media. Like some outlandish science-fiction film, the TV cameras came out of the woodwork as the first cars were torched and the first bricks thrown, in some cases even beating the police to the scene of the crime. From the very beginning of the King case, the infamous beating that Rodney endured from the four police officers subsequently put on trial was run and re-run by several TV networks—and most importantly, edited and re-edited to fit broadcasting schedules. Might the public have been artificially enraged by the constant replay of the tape, respliced to indicate a harsher beating than had actually occurred?

The "power of equality" to which Kiedis refers may well symbolize the most significant communicative power the world now has: the media. After all, another way in which the media played a role as instigators, averred Cannon and other commentators, is by televizing the violence itself: the constant flow of images depicting the police as powerless to defend against the rioters might well have encouraged more citizens to join in, and those already involved to redouble their efforts. However, this is a double-sided coin—on one occasion on that first afternoon of rioting, a live broadcast of the beating of a truck driver called Reginald Denny at the intersection of Florence and Normandie caused four local residents to run out of their houses and assist him.

Had Kiedis been able to look ahead a year to the riots, he might have intensified his lyrical attack still further. He certainly wouldn't have been impressed by the first response of the LAPD to the riots. LAPD chief Daryl Gates had chosen to attend a political fund-raising party in the wealthy beach community of Pacific Palisades, 20 miles from the center of the riots. The police department was understaffed and unprepared for an insurrection of this scale and pulled out of one of the hot spots (the aforementioned Florence and Normandie intersection) on the first day. This didn't help matters—the area quickly became a war zone. Fidel Lopez, a Guatemalan immigrant, was beaten to within an inch of his life, with the attack being captured on video. His assailants smashed a stereo speaker into his forehead, his genitals were spray-painted black and his body was doused with gasoline, presumably in order to set him on fire. However, his life was saved by a black clergyman who threw his body on Mr. Lopez's, persuaded the attackers to leave and then drove him to a hospital, when it had become clear that no ambulance crew would enter the area. Earlier that day, Choi Sai Choi, a Chinese book-keeper, had been dragged from his car, beaten and robbed at the same intersection. After some hours of destruction without a police presence, the National Guard was called in.

However, within hours of the first reports of violence and theft, the Bloods and the Crips gangs entered the fray, bringing a degree of motivation, organization, and firepower that was far beyond the scope of the average street thug.

Think the Chilis went over the top with "The Power Of Equality"? Think again. Things would get worse before they got better. The Los Angeles Fire Department reported that nine large stores were ablaze and that numerous cars had been deliberately torched in order to block the roads. A LAPD sergeant told reporters that the police department had called for a tactical recall, canceling leave for all officers. Many cops were patrolling the streets in full riot gear by this stage.

The song also comments on the white response to black anger: perhaps with the authorities in mind. Mayor Bradley wasn't standing for the stealing and other crimes, and declared a local state of emergency, with a night-time curfew in effect that would make a lockdown from dusk till dawn mandatory. He also prohibited firearms sales, banned petrol sales (unless it was loaded directly into vehicle fuel tanks), closed down all schools in southern LA, called in 2,000 extra National Guardsmen and arranged with President Bush for federal assistance to be invoked if required. At the end of the second day, an unidentified police officer commented to the news crews: "Things are totally out of control here... and we expect it to get worse when it gets dark. I hope we all live to see tomorrow."

The Chilis made grave—but accurate—predictions. By the time the riots in LA died down on May 4, the violence had spread to other cities, notably in San Francisco, where 1,400 people were arrested, with a state of emergency and curfew also in effect. In Las Vegas 200 rioters embarked on an arson and drive-by rampage. Downtown Seattle struck by mobs of up to 100 people, looting cars and attacking property. In New York, groups of up to 400 people stormed shopping malls. In Atlanta, police clashed with hundreds of black rioters. In Tampa, Pittsburgh, Omaha, and several other cities, black and Latino protesters demonstrated their sympathy with the LA rioters—either that, or a quick eye for an opportunity.

By the time the smoke had cleared, damage assessors were announcing that around a billion dollars of damage had been done to Los Angeles. Many thousands of arrests had been made, over 500 structures had been destroyed by fire, about 2,500 people had been injured and between 40 and 60 citizens had died (even ten years later the official body count varies, according to the source).

Songs such as "The Power Of Equality" can't solve problems: they just point to them. To this day no one has come to a simple conclusion about the LA riots—whether they represented the will of the people and were overall A Good Thing, or if they were the acts of an antisocial mob and therefore A Bad Thing. Too much information in favor of both arguments is available for either side to make total sense. But what we do have now is a sense of perspective on the riots. "Power Of Equality" was an early attempt to develop foresight before events spiraled out of control.

The issue of racism, endemic to a multicultural city like LA, was one that the Chilis felt strongly about. As Flea said, "Sometimes it's hard for me to see what's going on, because I never surround myself with anyone who has the slightest inkling of racism. It makes me so sick, I just wanna shit on their faces. There's definitely a monstrous racism problem. That's one of the main things we stand against, if we stand against anything." Kiedis added, "We stand very strongly for breaking down barriers. If people say this is too white for black radio, or too black for white radio, we just ignore them, because music is the last place we need bullshit racial barriers."

If You Have To Ask

"If You Have To Ask" is subtler on every level. A lighter, spiraling cut with Frusciante's organic, deliberately untreated guitar line sitting squarely on Flea's bassline, the song boasts a girlish falsetto from all the singers on the chorus line and is the polar opposite of heavier album tracks like "Suck My Kiss". It starts with a slight, chicken-scratch figure from Frusciante and a killer, tumbling bass riff from Flea broken up by the odd fretboard slide and his usual slinky fills. Frusciante's heavily wah-wah-laden solo is a pure Hendrix clone, accompanied by laughter and applause, while the bass brings the song to an elegant halt with a melodic cluster of notes. The lyrics are also much more vague than the polemics of the previous song, with the singer intoning, deadpan, image-heavy lines such as "Most in the race / Just lose their grace / The blackest hole / In all of space" and querying, "If you have to ask / You'll never know / Funky motherfuckers / Will not be told to go."

Breaking The Girl

A completely unexpected change in direction comes with the acoustic, anthemic "Breaking The Girl", which manages to be a rock tune—with all that implies: rambunctious chords, an uplifting, ascending chord sequence, a wall-of-sound pile of guitars—and a sensitive paean to something unidentified (but probably sexual) at the same time. Driven by several acoustic guitars, which together overwhelm Flea's understated bass part more than any more aggressive electric instruments elsewhere on the album, "Breaking..." is unique in the Chilis' canon, even by the standards of their current mellow, early-

Noughties direction. In fact, it's one of the first signs that the band could write chart-friendly hits as well as all-out dirty funk. Whether Kiedis is referring to a female relationship that didn't survive its circumstances, or a sexual act, or something metaphorical, is unknown. But there is genuine emotion implied by lines such as "We were the two / Our lives rearranged / Feeling so good that day / A feeling of love that day"—and witness the pain evident in whatever happened to make him sing, "She meant you no harm / Think you're so clever / But now you must sever / You're breaking the girl."

What makes "Breaking The Girl" so special is that it's a radical departure for the Chilis, and a sign of just how far they had come since the frat-boy "Party On Your Pussy" days. Lines of love-poetry such as this could only have come from a mind more developed than that. Perhaps the anti-jock wave of sentiment that had come from the grunge movement—the ultimate revenge-of-the-nerds scenario— had come a little early, and not from Seattle: from the valley of sin, Los Angeles. This was all the more bizarre coming from the buffed, slickly-styled Kiedis and his band of surf-punks, eminently cool to a man and quite the Hollywood party bunch.

Funky Monks

A stronger sense of wig-out fun was to be gained from "Funky Monks", a 1990s song ruined by a horrible noise-gated 1980s snare drum from Chad Smith. Also the title of a documentary shot and released on VHS the following year of the making of the album, the song is a simple, slow, funk workout with plenty of spaces between the instruments. It's a filler song, for sure—although it's a sign of this album's quality that even the fillers are fully-realized and disciplined, not just random jams—and nails an exquisitely economical groove to the floor, extending into an almost droned figure for the final minute before fading out in a jumble of live confusion, reminding the listener of the relaxed recording environment. Once again a falsetto vocal leads off the chorus, setting up a contrast between the super-masculine funk that the band push out. "You are on the road," wails Kiedis, almost vulnerably. "Can I get a little lovin' from you?". But as so often, he referred to sex: "Every man has certain needs / Talkin' 'bout them dirty deeds / To these needs I must concede." The juxtaposition between self-aware strength and self-declared weakness—truly the badge of the 1990s man-child pop star—is fully established by this stage in the album, just in time for the most bullish, gimme-some song here…

Suck My Kiss

The closest to a standard rock tune (with all that implies) that *BSSM* provides, the remarkable "Suck My Kiss" is—despite its sniggering title, designed to make listeners mistake it for something more graphic—an economical, funk-heavy tune whose greatest strength is its simplicity and precision. Opening with a background wail from Kiedis, the song is driven by a hefty main riff which marches until the chorus, which drops into a sudden, funky, stop-start chorus. A notable highlight of "Suck My Kiss" is the whole-band chord stabs that occur in the second half of each chorus with expert accuracy: in the first chorus the Chilis deliver three consecutive stabs, in the second chorus two, and in the final chorus just one—a feat of timing which anyone who has endured the hours of rehearsal that any band requires will admire.

"I am what I am / Most motherfuckers don't give a damn!" sneers Kiedis, adding, "Beware, take care / Most motherfuckers have a cold-ass stare." But it's the fairly specific chorus which lends the song its exciting, lewd, straightahead, and deliberate vulgarity, with the singer shouting in staccato stabs "Hit me you can't hurt me—suck my kiss / Kiss me please pervert me—stick with this... Your mouth was made to suck my kiss." As he explained to *Rolling Stone*, such explicit sexual overtures were meant positively rather than crudely. "I don't think our sexuality is belligerent; it's more a free-flowing musical display. And that's only one small part of who we are. If you made a list of every song that we've ever written, maybe ten percent would be sexually dominated. But I think that's the way the public is. If something's racy, they crave that, and they long to associate celebrities with those characteristics. People lust after provocative incidents. They love to talk about them over breakfast and mull over them while they're driving home from work."

As he explained, the sound and subject of funk (whose very name originates from an old slang term for genital odor) are inextricably connected: "The correlation between hard-core funk music and sexuality is so undeniable that to write about it and to sing about it seemed like the most natural thing in the world. So we did it, and we still do it. The fact that things are so different today because of the dangerous nature of sexual activity doesn't mean you have to cut out your sexuality. You just have to be more careful and more thoughtful."

He was referring to AIDS, which in the early 1990s was a threat taken more seriously than today (to the dismay of many present-day health authorities). Kiedis, known as a man who enjoyed sex and plenty of it, had much to say on the subject, musing: "I've been tested five times. I would never, ever want to give anybody I cared about—even someone I didn't care about—something that would kill them."

It was interesting to note that a public service advert for radio which the band had been asked to do the previous year had been pulled after the government agency that commissioned it discovered that Kiedis had a previous conviction for indecent exposure.

"Well, that's one of those stories where, from my point of view, everybody loses out," fumed Anthony. "This ad agency consigned by the government came to me and said, 'Will you do a radio PSA for the use of condoms?' And I said to myself, 'Well, that sounds like a very productive and positive thing to do.' So they come to our studio, and Flea and Chad and Dave play this sort of swinging jazz groove while I do this spiel about 'Here I am wearing my condom when I have sex, every time, not just when it's convenient, not just when my partner thinks of it, but every single time.' Which is something that everybody in the band believes in. And the ad agency was very pleased, and the government was very pleased. But then this woman who was in charge of the whole thing finds out that it's me and says, 'This guy did something to a girl'—which in reality I did not—and she was very rigid about getting me kicked off the program. The ironic fact was that I never did what it was that I was accused of."

He clarified: "Five years ago after a show in Virginia, this girl accused me of indecent exposure and sexual battery. I was guilty of the indecent exposure. And I told the judge that I didn't do it with the intention of hurting anybody—it was just a stupid prank. And maybe I learned something from that, which is, you cannot go around taking your dick out, because some people don't like it. But this thing where she claimed that I touched her, I just didn't do. I didn't get near her. We went to court, it was a very conservative county, and they convicted me of both things. It was shocking for me that a court of law could convict you of something you didn't do. But once you get into the court, anything can happen. It's her word against my word, with a bunch of very conservative jurors who are more likely to believe a girl who's going to college than a rock' n' roll boy who has a reputation for lewd activities... Like so many millions of other men on this planet, I love women. I love their essence and the way they think and the way they talk and the way they move and the way they feel. I don't think that's terribly unusual. Yes, I have a strong appreciation for women. But that doesn't mean I'm a womanizer."

I Could Have Lied
In fact, such amped-up male activities as womanizing seemed very far from the agenda in the next song, "I Could Have Lied"—a perfectly-sequenced riposte to "Suck My Kiss" in which the band show off their mellow side with great dexterity and restraint. A quietly strummed acoustic guitar underpins Kiedis's heartfelt crooning, the subject of which appears to be unrequited love, that standard theme. "There

must be something in the way I feel / That she don't want me to feel," he ponders, adding that if he'd lied he could have kept her: "I could never change just what I feel... The things I said to you were true... She struck me but I'm fucked-up now." Honesty not being the best policy is the unusual spin the band put on the subject, with this slight song giving Frusciante in particular the chance to fill the spaces with sweet, fingerpicked chords.

Mellowship Slinky In B Major

More standard funk material follows in "Mellowship Slinky In B Major" a roustabout, easy-to-digest chunk of riffage. Frusciante excels with subtle, one-note picking, while Kiedis's speedy raps contrast perfectly with P-Funk-derived shouts and Beach Boys-like woo-hoo backing vocals. Refreshingly, the guitarist uses heavy string-bending and a jangling, almost Eastern chord to create a middle-eight solo that is at odds stylistically with the rest of the song—once again a sign that the band cannot be predicted, even when they seem to be at their most predictable. A sweet descending piano figure can just be heard against the verse riff in the back half of the song, while Anthony intones, "Popcorn peanuts lookin' at big butts / No I can not keep my mouth shut," and giving shout-outs to his favorite sports team ("My Lakers I adore 'em") and to a famous artist ("Robert Williams, stroke and splatter / I attest to your gray matter"). Williams, the artist behind the picture which the Chilis' LA compatriots Guns N' Roses had used to adorn the cover of their debut album, 1987's *Appetite For Destruction*, was a suitably eccentric target for the band's adoration, having supported the punk movement for many years. Other cultural references include authors (Truman Capote, Charles Bukowski), actors ("Good God De Niro's insane"), and legendary jazz musicians ("Billie sings and Basie swings"), all of which makes the song, as Kiedis repeats, a slightly loaded take on "just a few of my favorite things."

The Righteous And The Wicked

Even to the Chilis' biggest fans, "The Righteous And The Wicked" can seem a little labored, with its over-earnest punk verse riff, the layered, almost progressive-rock midsection, and Frusciante's overuse of divebombed feedback. But there are interesting touches: in the main bass riff, Flea detunes his bottom string so that the note he plays on it is almost lower than human hearing can perceive, leading to a percussive thud that has almost no tone. Another "Power Of Equality"-style social commentary, the song refers to social ills such as war ("Kiss me we self-destruct … War and peace / The killing fist / Of the human beast"), the death of the planet ("Holy mother earth / Crying into space / Tears on her pretty face / For she has been raped"), abortion, and genocide. Perhaps a little piously, Kiedis ends his gloomy lament on a positive note, asking a hero for help ("Marvin Gaye my love / Where did we go wrong") and pleading for better times ahead ("Hear me when I'm calling you / From my knees / I am playing for a better day").

Give It Away

The album comes together more cohesively from this point. Given all the changes being rung around the Chilis and the new, softer approach which they were developing, it's ironic that one of the high points of *Blood Sugar Sex Magik* is the most obviously "Chili Pepper"-sounding song on it, the relentless "Give It Away". Plucked straight from the drawer marked *Mother's Milk*, the song was and remains the finest extant example of modern white funk to emerge in years. Nowadays the long-time Chilis fan will not be able to hear its opening salvo—a ringing, string-bend chord from Frusciante and Smith's staccato snare—without wincing. Like its big-rock-single contemporaries of the time—Nirvana's "Smells Like Teen Spirit" and Metallica's "Enter Sandman"— "Give It Away" has been a rock-club staple for so long that it inevitably evokes early 1990s images of rave culture, cute Daisy Age hip-hop hits and the rise of grunge: all about as cutting edge today as Slade.

But there's a reason why "Give It Away" has become such a benchmark: it is, without a doubt, one of the catchiest singles to be released in the last couple of decades. Once heard, it sticks irritatingly in the listener's ear and will not be removed. The core of this catchiness is twofold. Firstly, Flea's simple, elegant bass line—a simple upper-register slide with a three-note tail—is among his most effective work to date, taking the less-is-more philosophy that he had often spoken of introducing on the *BSSM* album to an elevated level. Only on two or three occasions does he drop in one of the squiggly fills for which he had become famous, making the whole effort a masterclass in economy.

Flea's reputation as a killer bass player had almost seen him lured away at one point. "John Lydon," Kiedis once reported, "once made a great stab at poaching Flea for Public

Image... And Malcolm McLaren tried to poach the whole band. He sat down with us, watched us rehearse, and then he said, 'OK, here's the plan, guys. We're going to simplify the music completely, so it's just basic, old-school, simple three-chord rock' n' roll, and we'll have Anthony be the focus of attention, and you guys will be the back-up band doing this surf-punk thing.' At which point Flea keeled over and passed out. It could have been what we had smoked—we were very dysfunctional at that point—but I think it was more what McLaren said."

Secondly, Kiedis's vocal—the closest to a rap, rather than singing, that he comes on this record—hangs on a repeated boast of "Give it away, give it away, give it away now," all of which he enunciates perfectly in couple of seconds at most. He adds a lip-flapping trill to the words "give it" in each case, leaving a slightly unnerving impression with the listener. It's a fantastic piece of vocal acrobatics and is all the more remarkable since Kiedis is not known for the speed or dexterity of his vocals, before or since.

As for the rest of the music, the song works well on all levels, especially with Frusciante's guitar part. Keeping his part unobtrusive for most of the song to allow Flea's flying bass to anchor the tune, John remains content to swipe gently at some funk chords in the background. When the chorus comes in he lets go a little more, but it's still clear that the band's aim was to drive the song with bass and vocals—and all four musicians achieve their goal admirably. Lyrically, Kiedis references all the right points, from the deliberately vague title theme (which he later defined as stemming from "giving away" as a useful maxim to live by) and Chilified icons such as Bob Marley.

The song made a profound impact. Kiedis later explained. "I was toy shopping in New York right before Christmas, and this little girl was tugging on her mom's coat, pointing at me and going, 'That's him, that's him.' And her mom came running over and said, 'Oh, I've just got to thank you, you've made my life so much easier.' She said the only way she could get her little girl dressed in the morning was to play our record and sing to her: 'Gimme an arm, gimme an arm, gimme an arm now.' And she puts her arm in the shirt, and then it's 'Gimme your leg, gimme your leg, gimme your leg now.' That happens a lot, with kids literally from the age of one. And to me, the appreciation of a child is the ultimate compliment."

With the singer aiming jibes at materialism ("Greedy little people in a sea of distress / Keep your more to receive your less") and invoking heroes ("Bob Marley poet and a prophet") and inviting all to share his message ("Come and drink it up from my fertility / Blessed with a bucket of lucky mobility"), the song is nothing less than a modern hippie anthem, and one that sounds perfect for the times in which it was created. Little wonder it remains a live anthem.

Blood Sugar Sex Magik

The tempo and the mood is taken down for "Blood Sugar Sex Magik" itself, a brooding, Captain Beefheart-growled mantra in which Flea, Frusciante and Smith are as tight as can be ("as tight as a haemorrhoid on a mosquito's ass" as Kiedis once crowed) and in which the singer delves deep into imagery. The central riff (announced by a drumbeat from Smith that is startlingly similar to that of Queen's "We

Will Rock You") is a slippery, wah-wah-loaded beast that strolls along under the verses but which blows up into a full-blown rock frenzy in the chorus, where Kiedis calls with supreme vigor, "Blood sugar baby / She's magik / Sex magik sex magik!" What does it mean? We can only assume that there's a woman—or the metaphor of womanhood—in there behind statements such as "Kissing her virginity, my affinity / I mingle with the gods, I mingle with divinity"). He also addresses the nature of pure lust—not a theme ever portrayed in a rock song with much taste or success, before or since—with the well-chosen, almost poetic words "Erotic shock is a function of lust, temporarily blind... / Uncontrollable notes from her snow-white throat / Fill a space in which two bodies float." Clearly Kiedis had evolved into a writer of some sensitivity since the funk-punk sentiments that had filled the previous Chilis albums.

Under The Bridge
Nowhere was this more apparent than the album's most-remembered song, "Under The Bridge"—the subject of endless debate since then and one of the most deceptive songs in the band's considerable canon. Its super-mellow, often-imitated intro sees Frusciante emulating Jimi Hendrix's life-affirming "Little Wing"—like that song, a perfect blend of clean lead and rhythm guitar) with a clutch of pulled-off, simple chords. The famous words "Sometimes I feel like I don't have a partner..." are heard from Kiedis, and this remarkable song begins.

The story behind the song was equally discussed in subsequent years, with its primary subject—that of "drawing blood" under a bridge—variously supposed to be a reference to a girl's first sexual experience, to a suicide attempt, or to the injection of mainlined narcotics. It wasn't until a couple of years later that Anthony Kiedis revealed which of these plausible subjects was in fact the truth, telling *Rolling Stone* about a low point he had reached at the nadir of his heroin addiction several years before. "I was reaching a demoralizing low, just kind of hanging out on the streets and doing my thing and not much else, sadly to say... I ran into some fairly unscrupulous characters involved with miniature Mafioso drug rings, and the hangout for one of these gangs was this particular location under a bridge. I ended up going there with this gang member, and the only way that I was allowed to go under this bridge was for him to tell everybody else that I was getting married to his sister. You had to be family to go there... That was one of just hundreds of predicaments that I found myself in, the kind that only drug addiction can bring about. It's not that [this] one place was more insidious than the other places. But that's just one day that sticks very vividly in my memory. Like, how could I let myself get to that point?" He refused to disclose the exact location of the bridge, saying merely: "It's downtown. But it's unimportant. I don't want people looking for it."

As to how the sorry subject had come to be made into a song so many years later, when Kiedis's life was so much healthier on so many different levels, he explained, "I was driving away from the rehearsal studio [in 1990] and thinking how I just wasn't making any connection with my friends or family, I didn't have a girlfriend, and Hillel [Slovak] wasn't there... The only thing I could grasp was this city." Los

Angeles itself (referred to in the lyrics as "this city of angels") was the friend who guided him through that moment of introspection, he mused, and became the principal agent of "Under The Bridge". "I grew up here for the last 20 years, and it was LA—the hills, the buildings, the people in it as a whole—that seemed to be looking out for me more than any human being. I just started singing this little song to myself: 'Sometimes I feel like I don't have a partner...' When I got home that day, I started thinking about my life and how sad it was right now. But no matter how sad or lonely I got, things were a million percent better than they were two years earlier when I was using drugs all the time. There was no comparison. I was reminding myself, OK, things might feel fucked-up right now, but I don't ever want to feel like I did two years ago."

The song itself isn't what most people expect a big hit to be: it doesn't have a big hook that radio stations could get excited about, and while it's melodic, it's wistful, minor-chord melodic—until the last section, when a full choir appears, aided by Frusciante's mother Gail and her friends. "It doesn't really have a hook," said Chad Smith. "And not to take away from Anthony, but he's not the greatest singer in the world. It's just cool and soulful. It's not like the guy who wins all the awards, Michael Bolton... But maybe that's why it's so great." The song's mystique lies, it seems, in this new and perhaps unique songwriting style: "In the end it wasn't like I was writing in any sort of pop-song format," said Kiedis. "I just started writing about the bridge—and the things that occurred under the bridge."

The song wasn't initially intended as a Chilis tune, producer Rick Rubin later explained. "Anthony Kiedis had shown me the lyrics when we were looking through his lyric book. I said, 'Oh, what's this?' and he said, 'It's a song I wrote, but it's not Chili Peppers.' He sang it to me and I thought it was beautiful. But he was emphatic: 'No, this isn't what we do!' I said, 'It's you, though, and what you, Anthony, and the Chili Peppers band create is what you do. It doesn't have to be limited to funk jams; you are allowed to do different things. It's just a question of 'Do you love the song?'

"What we do is really a big experiment, and there's no reason not to try different things," added Rubin later. "If it doesn't work, we all know it doesn't work. Usually. And we get in the habit of trying a lot of different things. You get everyone thinking in terms of 'nothing's in stone, there's the potential for more.' Usually. It's really a completely collaborative effort. Anyone who's got a good idea, if it makes the record better, we use it... Sometimes young artists, or insecure artists, hold on to things that don't matter because they feel, 'This is what makes me me.' They have this image that some little thing they do makes them what they are. But it doesn't."

In the song, Kiedis personifies the city, musing: "I drive on her streets / 'Cause she's my companion," and expressing his loneliness with the words "It's hard to believe / That there's nobody out there."

Most powerfully, he iterates, "Under the bridge downtown / Is where I drew some blood." His love for LA was obvious even when he talked about the song to the press, as was obvious when he told one East Coast interviewer who had expressed an interest in moving to California. "Don't. There are too many fuckin' New Yorkers here. Are you Catholic? Well, if you move here you have to promise you'll use birth control. We don't want you to breed." And yet the Chilis were the first to admit that the city of Los Angeles had its share of faults, with Frusciante saying of the Valley, where he grew up, "The Valley is the worst fuckin' place on the planet. Nothing but malls. Shopping is God. But I am glad I grew up there because I just locked myself in my room and played guitar."

Naked In The Rain

"Naked In The Rain" (not the first time a song of this title had appeared: for a moment one or two puzzled Chilis fans wondered if the band had covered the Blue Pearl techno hit of the year before) was back to the joyous funk territory. It's a fantastically evolved workout, with Flea not quite at the pyrotechnic heights of *Mother's Milk*—but as close as he ever got on this album, along with "Give It Away"—and a beautifully layered guitar marathon from Frusciante. As has been the Chilis' modus operandi twice already on *Blood Sugar Sex Magik*, a sudden falsetto chorus provides the butt-juggling impetus at which the band are so adept, while a remarkably raw, un-showoffy bass solo at its core showcases Flea's newfound, less-is-more approach.

As Flea recalled later, "I was trying to play simply on *Blood Sugar* because I had been playing too much prior to that, so I thought, I've really got to chill out and play half as many notes. When you play less, it's more exciting—there's more room for everything. If I do play something busy, it stands out, instead of the bass being a constant onslaught of notes. Space is good. it's not that I don't love the bass passionately any more—I just

The post-Hillel Slovak Red Hot Chili Peppers (clockwise from top left): guitarist John Frusciante, bassist Michael "Flea" Balzary, vocalist Anthony Kiedis, and drummer Chad Smith.

Sir Psycho Sexy himself: Anthony Kiedis in full flow.

Funkmaster extraordinaire Flea: the most talented bassist of his generation?

The talented, troubled John Frusciante: at his fiery peak with Blood Sugar Sex Magik.

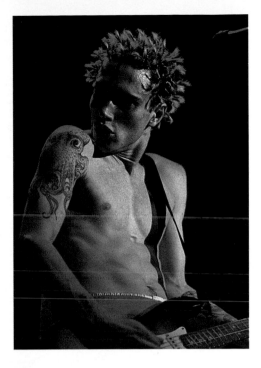

The "man's man" Chad Smith: the masculine foundation of the Chili Peppers

The 1985 Chilis, with drummer Jack Irons and guitarist Hillel Slovak (second and fourth from left).

Socks on cocks, onstage in Eindhoven, Holland in February 1988.

Taking sex magik to the masses: Hamburg, February 1992.

Frusciante: pre-meltdown in February 1992.

George Clinton –
early producer and
inspiration.

Producer Rick Rubin:
responsible for not one
but two Red Hot
Chili Peppers rebirths,
in 1991 and 1999.

The funkiest band in the world? Only time will tell...

felt I'd been getting too many accolades for being 'Joe Bass Player'... the whole concept of being a jack-off musician and not thinking about the big picture. I do consider myself fortunate to have achieved popularity as a bassist, but I felt there was too much emphasis being placed on playing technique, as opposed to just playing music. So before we recorded this album, I spent more time strumming an acoustic guitar than I did playing bass. To me, my bass parts are more incidental to the song now, because I'm thinking less as a bass player and more as a songwriter... [On Blood Sugar Sex Magik] I was coming out of a two-year period of misery, when I was down emotionally, physically and spiritually, [and] John played all his tracks once and maybe overdubbed a few solos, so the whole record was very spontaneous."

Rick Rubin had much to say on the subject, too, explaining: "When I started working with the Chili Peppers [on] the Blood Sugar Sex Magik album, up until that time Flea's bass playing was a particular style. He was famous for it, considered one of the best bass players in the world because of it. But when we started working together, that bass playing that made him one of the best didn't necessarily serve the songs in the best way. It was more about the bass being great. And, the song is more important than the bass. I think, starting with that record, he changed the way he played. Not that it was so different stylistically, but it was more about playing the parts that supported the song. Instead of playing the parts that he liked the best or that were the coolest. It was a very interesting part of the change in the Chili Peppers' sound, from being a, let's say, traditional funk band to being more of a songwriting band."

Thematically, "Naked In The Rain" seems to be merely a paean to wild, natural living, whether physically or as metaphor. Kiedis semi-raps, "Cold and mean people give me the creeps... Losing my taste for the human race...". A touch of misanthropy perhaps, especially when allied to the "global abortion" image brought up earlier—but one which makes this multilayered album so much more rounded. After all, if the overall message of *Blood Sugar Sex Magik* is one of love and affection, it wouldn't be strictly human (of this most human of bands) if a little negativity wasn't also part of the recipe.

Apache Rose Peacock

"Apache Rose Peacock" is a complex slab of pop-funk with a rollicking, almost nursery-rhyme chorus lifted by Kiedis's spiralling vocal hook ("Yes my favorite place to be / Is not a land called Honalee"). The story of the singer's mystical encounter with a beautiful girl—aided by the spirit of Louis Armstrong— the song is aided by Flea's muted and jazz trumpet and the pure Prince snicker of Frusciante's guitar. The main riff is a phenomenally tight interplay between the bass and guitar, itself worth the attention of any Chilis fan, before the sparky chorus and unexpected time-signature change emerges in the middle. Kiedis builds the scene colorfully: "Lunatics on pogo sticks / Another southern fried freak on a crucifix" before describing his paramour with panache: "I saw a bird walkin' down the block named Apache Rose Peacock / I could not speak, I was in shock / I told my knees to please not knock...". The song ends in a bustle of technicolor pictures, with Kiedis gleefully concluding: "Voodoo gurus casting their spells... Flowing like a flame all through the night / My girl's insane but it's all right."

"Apache Rose Peacock" is notable for a harder, almost metallic, riff that fills the last 30 seconds, presaging the much harder punk-funk that follows it of "The Greeting Song", perhaps the most hard-hitting song on the album and a direct response to the mellow tones of "Breaking The Girl" and "Under The Bridge". The most lyrically ambiguous song on the record—other than for its good-time ethos—it's notable for the organic tones (some of the backing vocals are noticeably off-key) and the enormous energy that flows through it, despite Flea's later statement that at the time of recording he had just emerged from a period of immense sadness.

My Lovely Man

Perhaps all this good-time lyrical self-amusement is intended as a preface to the most introspective song on the record, "My Lovely Man", a tribute to the departed Hillel Slovak and—despite its Hendrix-like, upbeat funkiness—dripping with the anguish Kiedis feels for his dead friend. Inspiration came from deep within, as he explained. "'My Lovely Man' is about my love for Hillel and the fact that eventually I will find him," he said. "It's kind of like when I die, I am counting on him to save me a seat. And whenever I sing that song, Hillel is completely in my world.

"Especially living in the city of Los Angeles and doing what I do, it's very easy to get wrapped up like an onion with millions of layers of bullshit and completely lose touch with your inner core. You forget you're just a person with these real feelings of love and sadness and happiness and horniness and pleasure. You just kind of go through life like a rolling fucking snowball, picking up more layers as you go along.

Every now and then, I need to get reminded that I'm just a person with these feelings.

"The other day, I [had] about 40 appointments, and I'm answering a million phone calls and opening letters and packages, and I got this package in the mail from this girl who's been a friend of mine for years, who had been holding onto this box for me, this little brown-paper box which Hillel had given me in 1986. There was something written on the box and it said: 'Anthony, you think what I feel and understand what I say. I love you. This is our year, 24. Hillel'... I went out into my back yard, and I just sat there for a minute, and all of a sudden, I managed to get through all of those layers, and I got down to the real me. I started crying to myself—and talking to Hillel."

Asked by *Rolling Stone* if subconsciously the band would never accept another guitarist as Slovak's equal, the singer explained—in the deadpan, detached style that people had come to realize meant that he was struggling to communicate—"Subconsciously and consciously, that's very true. Nothing will ever be like Hillel, Flea and Anthony as a trio. That's impossible. That was a point in our lives both musically and personally that will never be repeated, and it's insane to think that it ever would be. But I think we dealt with that realisation a long time ago." A side point to note here is that Frusciante, a member of a band whom he worshipped, would have been dealing with this second-league status—however amicably meant and honestly expressed—along with the other issues that were beginning to affect him during the recording of the album. Who knows how much such comments affected him, when his paranoia started to bite?

Flea said once that a sad side-effect of losing Slovak was that the band's in-jokes were lost with him. Kiedis makes reference to this with "I used to shout across the room to you / And you'd come dancin' like a fool / Shuffle step you funky mother"—the loss of the familiar quirks and personal traits of his friend must have haunted him. When Kiedis, Flea and Slovak were students at Fairfax High School in Hollywood, they had formed a joke band called Los Faces, which didn't play music but involved hour-long discussions in Cheech and Chong voices. "The inside jokes we had between us just from sitting around and being silly, died with him," Flea added.

Worse, Kiedis had not—at least by this stage in the Chilis' career—come to terms that Slovak's death could just as easily have been his own. "It should have been me," he mourned. "My propensity for over-the-edge indulgences was more renowned then his. When Flea got the phone call, his first reaction was 'Anthony's dead'... Hillel was the closest person to me in my life, and sadly enough, I don't think I can ever find that with anybody else, because I don't think it happens more than once that you get that close to somebody. But as close as we were, because we were both afflicted with this disease of drug addiction, we didn't really hang out together because we didn't like to see each other in that state." The song ends, sadly but hopefully, with the lines "I love you too / See my heart / It's black and blue / When I die / I will find you".

Sir Psycho Sexy

Blood Sugar Sex Magik ends with a slow funk workout entitled "Sir Psycho Sexy", a flashback to the *Freaky Styley* P-Funk days—comedy vocals, super-slippery bass (aided by an envelope filter, autowah and whatever other outlandish funk effects Flea had dialled up) and the sex-and-more-sex obsessions that had made the band so recognizable. Kiedis is on hyper form, laconically spitting out the lines, "Deep inside the garden of Eden / Standing there with my hard-on bleedin' / There's a devil in my dick and some demons in my semen…". He was at his most explicit on this song, adding, "That cop she was all dressed in blue… I said what's up, now suck my dick… I could feel her getting wet through her uniform…." Despite the rampant lyrics, the music of the song is both sensitive and sweet, with a beautiful descending sequence introduced in the song's middle section and extending as a coda at its end. The strings in particular—if they're synthesized or real is hard to tell, and not really relevant—lend the end of the song a grace that suits this epic, landscaped album.

They're Red Hot
But the band aren't quite finished, tacking on a ramshackle—but supertight—cover of blues legend Robert Johnson's "They're Red Hot" at the end. Recorded at triple speed and notable for Flea's delightful walking bass line and Smith's ridiculous polka-style beat. Johnson—the master of blues innuendo—laughs down the 20th century at us as the band wade through his song, barely more than a minute in length, with the words: "You know the monkey, now the baboon playin' in the grass / Well, the monkey stuck his finger in that old Good Gulf Gas, now…" between the frantic choruses. Famously, this song was recorded outdoors, and the sounds of the nearby LA freeway can be heard in the background.

The band had tired of the recording studio and simply lifted their instruments and recording equipment lock, stock and barrel out of the door.

And so *Blood Sugar Sex Magik* comes to a close.

When the album appeared, it was wrapped in an eyecatching sleeve. Composed of a graphic layout of the four bandmembers' heads on each side of the square cover, with snake-like tongues added and joining in the centre of the design, the record couldn't help but attract attention. The Chilis dedicated their masterpiece to Mike Watt, sometime bassist with LA punk legends the Minutemen and later Firehose—a bow to the punk scene in the city that had inspired them with bands such as Black Flag, The Screamers, The Weirdos, and The Germs.

A true pioneer of polemical, aggressive punk music, Watt had calmed down a little since his Minutemen days by the time that *BSSM* was dedicated to him, but the Chilis knew how important a cultural mover he still was. There was a personal link to the band too—the very first Chili Peppers concert had taken place supporting the Minutemen, with the old Hillel Slovak line-up.

Watt recalled of the Chilis, "Their first gig was with the Minutemen, way back when Hillel was in the band, Flea, and Anthony. It's a trip how things go on, but still just people, which is good… if [people] change, and get full of themselves, then that's just kinda sad. But I'm happy to say they never did."

Whether or not the dedication to him meant much to him is unknown, although it's safe to assume that with the two bands' shared history, he was touched—even though he wasn't too informed about the newest rock bands of the day, as he admitted. "I don't know a lot of the younger bands. I was in a video for a band called Good Charlotte. I had never heard of 'em, but they were nice guys. I played a jury foreman. The whole scene kinda changed in some ways. But there's still some of the old spirit too—young guys who just wanna make bands and put on their own shows. But then there's the other side too, how it became mainstream, which was a big surprise for those bands—Green Day and stuff. It was a big surprise for me, too.

"I thought [punk would] always be a fringe thing. I never thought real young people would be into it. Even in the 1980s, when the young people started getting into the hardcore scene, I still thought it was a fringe thing. When [I] graduated high school, we could never have imagined that punk would become like a regular phase that teenagers go through. Back then, it was more like the glam and glitter thing."

The last words on *Blood Sugar Sex Magik* go to Flea and Anthony Kiedis. "We're proud," said the bass player. "We're proud of every note in every song."

And Kiedis told *Rolling Stone*, "We lived in this house for two months and never fought. We were just so happy to be making this record. And when we finished it, it was the greatest sense of accomplishment that we'll probably ever know. We knew it was a watershed for us."

the rise, fall and rise

What happened to the Red Hot Chili Peppers after they made BSSM

Blood Sugar Sex Magik was a huge international hit on its release in September 1991, hitting No. 3 on the US *Billboard* album chart and scoring highly in many dozens of countries. It eventually went on to sell almost nine million copies, the majority of those in the US, where its impact and those of its attendant singles were felt most keenly. The band released the singles "Under The Bridge" (US No. 2 / UK No. 26, reissued No. 13), "Breaking The Girl" (US No. 15 / UK No. 41), and "Give It Away" (US No. 1 / UK No. 9) internationally, and "Suck My Kiss" (No. 15) in the US only—quite a parade of chart success for a band which had previously scored only lower-chart hits. Accompanied by a parade of technicolor videos and the *Funky Monks* video-cassette of the recording of the album, the music of the Chili Peppers seemed to be everywhere for a period of three years or so—finally finding its milieu where before it had never quite seemed to fit in.

Funky Monks in particular is the essential guide for anyone who wants to know exactly what it was like to record the album in that most unorthodox of studios, the haunted mansion in Laurel Canyon. With a narratorless drive that is commonplace nowadays but which in 1991 seemed a pioneering move, the film shows the band in all their human frailty—and conversely, Rubin as an impassive guru. Kiedis is refreshingly honest about the inspiration behind "Under The Bridge", Frusciante—who seems withdrawn at the end of the movie—discusses masturbation and the others talk animatedly about their music.

The media had much to say on the album. *The Observer* noted somewhat snootily, "On the Chilis' fifth album, *Blood Sugar Sex Magik*, they propound a hazy philosophy in which lusty hedonism and New Age spirituality are conflated. Their back-to-nature rhetoric carries through to an interest in tribalism and an admiration for American-Indian folk ways." *Rolling Stone* talked of Rubin's streamlining of the band's previously chaotic sound, and Q magazine made much of the razor-sharp precision of the rhythm section. Overall, it seemed, the world's reviewers were pleased with the Chilis' latest work—although their reaction would be elevated further as singles success, and touring acclaim, gave the album an even bigger and brighter aura.

By the end of 1991 the Red Hot Chili Peppers had embarked on a lengthy tour to promote the album. Initial dates went well, although Frusciante later admitted that he had been troubled for some time: "I felt like a guy with 400 ghosts telling him what to do all the time," he said. "I just wanted to lay back on the couch and think about nothing, and that's what I did till I went on tour, aside from one miserable two-week European interview thing. It just had to do with my subconscious and my development as a person and spirit." As the inner voices increased and his general feeling of sadness at the state of his life and band grew, he began to find it difficult to face his bandmates, particularly Anthony. "The unity hadn't been good with the band for ages. Anthony and I hadn't talked for a couple of tours, and we didn't look at each other much onstage. So Flea took me to the park and said, 'Is there anything you like about being in the band?' and I said, 'No, I'm just in the band because I love you. I love playing with you, and I don't want to just leave you, but there's nothing I like about being in the band.' And he said, 'I guess you shouldn't do it just for me.' He understood, but he didn't think about it for the next year."

"I'd done a lot of thinking and I wasn't very social," he explained later. "I felt like I was turning my brain inside out to where my subconscious was becoming my conscious. I was understanding things that a man doesn't have a right to understand, about the way people's energies work together, and who they are. Why a rock star makes one person happy and another makes you... wanna kill them. I was seeing these things in a way that was... disgusting. Really disgusting. I could deal with it until I saw the depths. At that point, everything that was beautiful to me became ugly. Everything that had previously brought me happiness caused me the hugest sadness. Music. Paintings. People. It was pure depression. [Heroin] caused these things to be beautiful again."

This had not gone unnoticed by this most fraternal of bands, with Kiedis pondering with the benefit of hindsight, "[He] didn't seem happy on the road. We could tell there was an unpleasant tension with him." Chad Smith also recalled, ruefully: "We should have seen it coming, you know. John was 18 or 19 at the time. He had no experience of what it was like to play in a band, let alone a band like the Red Hot Chili Peppers. I'm a huge Zeppelin fan, and I think I would have freaked as well if I would have been asked to join Led

Zeppelin as a drummer. It was pretty obvious that it couldn't work out. We just didn't see it at the time."

Drugs were the logical escape, in particular heroin, which provides a powerful barrier between the user and his environment. "When I was in the band I'd take heroin every now and then, but it wasn't a problem," said Frusciante. "I was smoking pot night and day and I went through the world thinking it should be the way I believe it should be. And if it's not like that then I'll shut that part of the world out. I was scared I'd lose my ability to be creative. I thought being a heroin addict and making my life nothing but good feelings was the best way to maintain being a creative person. But it's not."

The end came quickly. In early 1992, John told his bandmates that he was leaving the Chilis—in mid-tour, presenting a hellish sequence of logistical problems. The band, he explained, was just too big and too popular for him to handle. "When I quit it was a shock. To them, it seemed like it was getting better as far as the [bandmembers] getting along went. But I didn't wanna do it any more. I was really happy, like my own version of happy, in outer space every time I would look at Flea's eyes, or my amp, or Chad's foot. But the popularity thing bummed me out."

What had started as hero-worship was soon sullied by reality, he said. "I expected them to be perfect and when they weren't I got mad at them. I'd get angry at Anthony and fight a lot with Flea. We'd say rude things back and forth to each other. I never really got over that feeling for the first four years I was in the band. Of course we were friends and loved each other, but when you start out with such an artificial image of somebody, it's hard to balance that out with seeing them as they truly are."

He added, "When I joined the band, I wanted nothing more in life than to be a rock star. It was what I was working for and everything I wanted. So for the first couple of years I very superficially dedicated myself to that: getting drunk, getting together with girls, and not being true to myself. Then at a certain point I completely changed. I started dedicating myself to being the best musician I knew how, and it completely threw me off balance. I started to hate being a rock star. The last couple of years I was in the band I really hated interviews, photo sessions, and fans asking for autographs... I saw death in everything around me... and everything that was beautiful represented everything that was sad, lost and gone. I couldn't listen to music, read books, or watch movies any more; I couldn't do anything and I didn't want to think. Everything made me miserable and all I could do was lie on the couch and stare vacantly into space."

Kiedis was on the phone in his hotel room, talking to an interviewer in New Zealand, when Flea came in to break the news. As he later recalled, "Flea looked at me with this completely puzzled and surreal, sad face. He said, 'John wants to quit the band and go home right now.' It stunned me and it shattered me because things had been going so well" (the "getting along" to which Frusciante had referred). A band meeting was called and the guitarist presented his case to his stunned colleagues. "I could tell by the look in his eye that he was really serious," Kiedis remembered. "He said, 'I can't stay in the band any more. I've reached a state where I can't do justice to what we've created, because of stress and fatigue. I can't give what it takes to be in this band any more.'"

"We kept a positive face on the operation," Kiedis added, "hoping that it was going to work out. He's one of the most deeply soulful guitar players that we've ever been connected with. Also, he's a good friend, and we had something going that was cosmic and special. And we're going to have to find that elsewhere." The singer, who had his own demons to wrestle with but whose strength and confidence seemed to be greater than that of Frusciante, was enjoying the band's newfound success since *Blood Sugar Sex Magik*, telling *Rolling Stone*, "We've never succumbed to the pressures of management or agents or record companies wanting us to work harder and tour longer and make more records. We know we wouldn't be happy doing that. In order for us to have the juice to make music, we have to live our lives in other ways. We'd be empty if all we ever did was tour and record."

And, ironically, where the guitarist had buckled under the pressure of seeing his band go from medium to huge inside a single year, Kiedis viewed this rise as slow enough to cope with. "For years, Flea and I roamed around the city not having any idea how we were going to go about eating lunch or dinner," he explained. "When we first hooked up with our manager, we said, 'If you want to manage us, you have to make sure that we eat every day.' That was the big thing. We never had money of our own or houses or cars or anything like that. But in the last few years, everything's changed drastically. We made a lot of money, we all bought houses and cars, and we can take care of our families. I just bought my father a house; I take care of my mother; and I take care of my sisters. I put my sisters through college last year. That's a huge change for me, being able to take care of my family and help my friends out if they need any help. That's a strange loss of tension in our lives... because our ascent was so gradual, we had a lot of time to figure out how we were most comfortable doing what we do. If we'd become tremendously popular after our first record, I think we would've disintegrated years ago. But because it happened over the course of five records, we had a lot of time to figure it out along the way."

"Success is different to a lot of different people," he added later. "I think that we were successful from the very first day we became a band, because we were doing something that we believed in. Playing music for people, whether it's two people or two million people, is being successful."

"I'm all for us getting a bunch of money," Flea added, "but it's not a priority. Our mental health comes first. I already feel like the richest man in the world. I've got a place to live, a car, loads of food and clothes, and I get given everything for doing what I love. This band's the best thing that has ever happened to me."

The bass player looked back on it all with pleasure, once the dust had settled. "It was a very intense year. We were able to communicate with a large number of people without changing, and we made a lot of money. Now I can take my friends out to eat whenever I want, and not have to skip out the back door. It's completely insane how one song can make such a difference," he added, referring to "Under The Bridge".

Inevitably, the success of BSSM had been followed in short order by the opportunity for the bandmembers to branch out into different areas of activity, with one notable example being Kiedis's resumption of acting in the film *Point Break*, a no-brain thriller that paired Keanu Reeves and Patrick Swayze in the most satisfying, and simultaneously most stupid, surf movie ever made. Kiedis played a generic thug. But this was not to last, as he explained later. "Right now the most important thing in our artistic careers is being the Red Hot Chili Peppers. We all have other interests, and sometimes we experiment with doing movies or producing other records or fiddling around on a Sunday afternoon at the park with our children. But as far as being creative people, this is the most important thing in the world to us right now. We have a lot on our plate as the Red Hot Chili Peppers and it's all we can do to maintain focus and accomplish what we're trying to do, which is play music."

Frusciante bid his colleagues farewell and took a plane home from Japan, where the band were playing a mini-tour at the time. But peace of mind still didn't come. "There were things taking place inside of me that were very confusing to me," he recalled later. "I had all these voices in my head all the time, which I still do, but at that time I wasn't spiritually protected against the spirits that meant me no good. Ghosts that are just there to fuck with me and drive me crazy. I couldn't discern between them and the ones that were helping me and I was so confused. Everything that I was learning seemed to be pulling me more towards death."

Like many people with psychological problems exacerbated by drug use, the inner turmoil simply grew and grew. "The voices had been telling me to quit the band ever since we finished *Blood Sugar Sex Magik*," he added. "But at that time there seemed that there was no reason to quit the band.

Other than I had a funny feeling about what going on tour was going to do to me as a creative person—because at that point I was still growing creatively—but once we went on tour, I stopped growing and started coming apart."

Frusciante could neither handle being in the Red Hot Chili Peppers nor being out of them, it seemed. "I was totally incapable of it: I had just so many mental problems. It wasn't until I was 28 that my brain actually felt like a spacious place. When I was 18, 19, 22, my brain was just clogged all the time—non-stop voices. I couldn't figure out what was going on. There was a lot of confusion inside me, this flood of voices, often contradicting each other, often telling me stuff that would happen in the future, and then it would happen, voices insulting me, telling me what to do. I might have made things a bit more balanced if my head had been a little clearer, but it wasn't, with the amount of pot I smoked—24 hours a day by the time I was 20. I had this feeling that there was something else I needed to do for myself on the inside that had nothing to do with my outward presentation to the world, so playing live in the Chili Peppers was making me severely depressed. If I had quit at the end of *Blood Sugar Sex Magik*, I think I could have gone through this stuff easier, without becoming a drug addict. But by the time I did leave, hard drugs were the only way I could be happy enough to live and not just be the most hopeless person who can't even listen to music and is about to die."

One last decision remained. "I took a clear-cut decision that I was going to be a drug addict. All of the thoughts in my head had resolved into something that I was calling 'the will to death'. Everything made me miserable, so I made the decision one day that I was gonna be on heroin and cocaine all the time, because when I was on them was the only time I was happy. So I figured there was no disadvantage in it and nobody could talk me out of it. During that period of time I had a lot of communication with what you might call ghosts in many different forms. It was such a fun time, I definitely got something in return for all the belief that I'd had in those things before I ever saw them for real."

And so John Frusciante's descent into hell began.

Meanwhile, Kiedis, Flea, and Smith had regrouped and, despite their shock and grief at what had transpired, were determined to battle onwards. Within a matter of days a new guitarist, Arik Marshall, had been recruited and was in the rehearsal room mastering Frusciante's parts. The tour continued successfully and the Chilis completed two years on the road. Despite the personnel shuffles, the later tour— which included a stint on 1992's Lollopalooza event— turned out fine. As Flea recalled, "It was definitely a situation for kids who didn't want to go see the same old boring shit. They could spend a whole day there, have a party, and see all different kinds of music. It was a totally positive, beautiful thing."

When the time came to lay off the constant touring and record some new material, Marshall was found to be lacking the vital ingredient as an in-studio Chili Pepper and left. He was briefly replaced by Jesse Tobias, but this guitarist was no more useful than his predecessor and the band only achieved a measure of stability with the recruitment of ex-Jane's Addiction axeman Dave Navarro, also a sporadically lapsing heroin user and a man of enormous creativity. Navarro's first show as a Chili Pepper came when the band headlined Woodstock 94. Flea enthused, "For us, playing Woodstock was a very exciting experience. I think we went there really questioning the whole thing, questioning the fact that they were advertising peace and love and at the same time it seemed to be about corporate structures and merchandising But when we got to play, the energy of the whole thing really took over. There were zillions of people having a great time and it was our first show with Dave and we were really excited and we had a fun time."

By this stage the Red Hot Chili Peppers were one of the biggest bands in the world, alongside REM, U2, Guns N' Roses and Metallica. The first fruits of the new line-up came in 1995, with a new album entitled *One Hot Minute*. Although the band were on fine form and Rick Rubin was once again at the helm, the record failed to match the pyrotechnic glories of its predecessor—perhaps not because of its quality but because times had changed. After all, the nu-metal generation had been born with Korn's debut album the year before, and downtuned, angry darkness, not psychedelic funk, was becoming more and more the order of the day.

At the time, however, optimism was running high in the Chilis camp. Navarro and the band were enjoying life and had no reason to suppose that the new album would not equal *Blood Sugar Sex Magik*. Kiedis talked earnestly of the mutual respect that existed between the bandmembers—for all the world as if it was still 1991. "Obviously it takes a whole lot of love and a lot of friendship and a lot of learning for a band to stay together [as long as we have] and to constantly do something different with every record. I think without a genuine love for each other, we would have dried up a long time ago as a band. There have been tragedies and incredibly inspirational experiences along the way, but the one thread that has been consistent has been the desire to create something honest, soulful and powerful. When we were making music 12 years ago, we were making it because it felt good and we wanted to do it, and we're still making music because it feels good and we want to do it."

Smith amplified this. "We really feel that we've grown and changed by learning about ourselves and learning about our lives and trying to become more kind, sensitive people and that's all reflected on our new record. This band is not based on strangers coming together to make music. It's based on friends sharing their lives. That's who we are, and without that friendship I don't think we would exist at all."

Asked about his forecast for the success of *One Hot Minute*, Flea responded, "The commercial success of a record is really not our concern. Our concern is trying to make the most honest music that we can. We're really proud of this record. We think we've grown a lot and made an album that sounds different than anything we've ever done. And whatever the world wants to do with it is fine. We hope that we can communicate to as many people as possible because we have love to give the world. We're not really concerned with what other people think about us. Our only concerns are just progressing artistically..."

Where the band had been cagey but basically compliant when it came to talking about song themes at the time of release of *Blood Sugar Sex Magik*, this time around they were mulishly stubborn. "I hate talking about songs," intoned the always-distant Kiedis. "I really hate analyzing our music. It takes all the fun out of it. It takes the mystery and the beauty out of it. We work on songs and record them for people to hear and it isn't our place to sit there and try to give detailed explanations of how a song came to be or what it's about."

Flea added, more graciously, "Being misunderstood is sort of par for the course, at least for us. I think probably because of certain things we've done in our career, there have been a lot of misconceptions about this band. There have been misconceptions that we're just a party band from California that surfs and skates all the time and that all of our songs are about that. I think that's a very common misconception. I think the Red Hot Chili Peppers have always run a pretty wide spectrum throughout our careers, and obviously through the years we have become more capable to express that range. But, you know, people can think what they will. We don't regret anything; we're proud of everything we do."

But the ghost of *Blood Sugar Sex Magik*—a terrible sword of Damocles marked "Can you do better next time?" hanging over them—wouldn't go away, as evidenced in Kiedis's defiant statement that "For the last record, *Blood Sugar Sex Magik*, we all moved into a house and lived together while we recorded. But I think it would be pretty stupid to try to recreate something we did a long time ago, so we tried to do something new this time. We went to Hawaii for three months and lived and wrote songs and played around together... Songwriting is a state of mind, it's a state of spirit. It happens every way imaginable. There's no formula. No song is ever written the same way twice. It happens with a bass line. It happens with a guitar part. It happens with a drum part. It happens with a vocal part. It happens when we get together and work and there is no secret to it. It's just an intangible factor of illogical behavior. And then some."

Psychologically, however, things were generally more settled now that Frusciante had retreated into seclusion. For example, although the family backgrounds of both singer and bassist had been complex, not to say destructive, by this stage in their careers the bandmembers were talking positively about their relatives. "I think all of our parents love what we do and completely support us," Kiedis averred. "They come to our shows and we've even had the privilege of Flea's grandmother sitting on stage while we play."

Flea added: "They were proud of us before we were in a band and before we had the commercial success that society places so much emphasis on. They just wanted us to be happy whatever we did, as long as we didn't hurt ourselves or anybody else."

Signing off on the unloved *One Hot Minute*, it was apparent that the reconstructed 1960s hippie vibe that the band had retained three decades after the movement's peak was still flourishing. "We've always been emotionally diverse," Kiedis concluded. "I think that the longer that we're alive, the more aware of ourselves we become and that gives us the ability to express ourselves more clearly. It's always been there and it's just what people are able to connect with from the outside in."

"All there is in life is honesty and love," Flea chipped in. "There's nothing else, really, and without those, we simply couldn't exist. It would just be ridiculous."

Even the new boy Navarro threw in some pure LA rock-star-speak with "I think we all relate to each other in our personal experiences, whether they be joyous and happy or traumatic and sad, and that's what this album is. It's a combination of all our personal experiences thrown into the mix to create a beautiful and wonderful combination."

In the same year, 1995, John Frusciante resurfaced to a degree with a solo album, the obscure *Niandra Lades And Usually Just A T-Shirt*, an eclectic collection of songs which was his final farewell to his old band. As he said, "The last thing on it was recorded right before I quit the band, and it's the sound of somebody falling apart. I had to do a shift of reality. I had to figure out what was going on inside of me and go on an adventure to find out what it was that I was looking for, because I was very sad by that time."

By this point his deadly heroin and cocaine addiction had taken hold. "It got to the point where there was no one looking at me the way people look at you when you're famous, with that love even though they don't know you. I was getting physical pain. I felt like childhood traumas that I had never even felt existed were now coming up to get me. This life that we're trussed into when we become rock stars acts as a kind of doctor for us and we don't even realize that it's happening. We just take it for granted."

Much later on, he looked back on the experience with more perspective. "It was too high, too far, too soon. Everything happened—or better, everything *seemed* to be happening—at once and I just couldn't cope with it. I really don't know how it all happened. There wasn't a single incident where I could put my finger on it and say, 'This was it.' It was just hard for me to cope with it all. You've got to remember that I was an absolute Red Hot Chili Peppers fan. Their music meant everything to me, and all of a sudden I was a part of them. They called me 'Greenie' because I was the youngest, but that didn't do it. I don't know what did it. I probably tried to fit in, make experiences the others made in a long time in a short time."

As Flea said: "We were never a band that promoted a clean and healthy lifestyle... I had drug problems. Anthony was a junkie. We were all battling with our addictions. It is easy to get sucked into this lifestyle, and I guess that's what happened to John. He was too young and inexperienced to deal with it all. We were older and knew the game and [still] had a hard time dealing with it. But drugs weren't just a part of the band: somehow we grew up in Hollywood and drugs were part of the whole rock culture. They just suck you in."

Things got worse. In 1997, as the Chilis licked their wounds after the reception of the unprepossessing *One Hot Minute*, Frusciante's life was becoming less and less vital. He released a second solo album, *Smile From The Streets You Hold*, despite his hellish addiction a sweet, emotional record—but one that, he later admitted, had been recorded solely to raise money for drugs. At this point he was injecting cocaine every few minutes, as he later told one interviewer.

This hadn't escaped the Hollywood rumor mill, and it was known that he was on a downhill route towards joining his predecessor, Hillel Slovak, in the club reserved for those who die young from drugs and despair. In the same year, an LA reporter tracked him down to his room in the Chateau Marmont hotel and broke the story that he was in terrible shape: he had lost most of his front teeth, his skin and hair were in awful condition, his fingernails were covered with dried blood and his body was covered with abscesses from infected injection sites.

And yet he remained mentally positive, not caring about his physical condition in favor of his mental wellbeing—in other words his avoidance of reality. "I'd totally lost balance in that way," John said later. "It was all about what I felt mentally. I did get through it really well, and I attribute that to my not caring and not feeling bad about it. I felt I was doing something good and healthy for myself and I didn't care if people said it was unhealthy. Most other junkies that I knew felt really guilty about it, but I always felt that I was doing something good." He reported later that when he felt near death during his heroin addiction, he was visited often by spirits. "I was so happy someone was visiting, I'd make food for them," he explained. "When they were gone, I'd cry."

The clock was ticking, but didn't stop in the way that some expected. Remarkably, Frusciante claimed much later on that he knew all along how long his addiction was going to last. "Voices in my head had been counting me down ever since I started," he said. "At the beginning they said, 'You can go on drugs for six years now.' And two years before I quit I remember a voice in my head saying, 'You can still do drugs for another two years and then you're gonna quit.'"

The moment came—and passed. "At the point where I stopped I knew that if I kept doing them I was gonna die. I probably had like three months," he reported. "That was what the voice in my head was saying, and I also knew that a lot of these spirits were truly on my side and wanted me to stop at that point. They'd always been in favor of me doing it, and suddenly, they all wanted me to stop. So I had no doubt in my mind that I was doing the right thing."

To the utter surprise of those few who still knew Frusciante, he decided to clean up his act. Checking himself into a rehabilitation facility and apparently conquering his inner fears, Frusciante emerged into the outside world. "When I finally stopped for good," he pondered, "I felt very sure of myself and I knew it was the right time... I have a great will to live because of what I think I'm doing by living here. I think I'm taking care of things in other dimensions by being here. I see this three-dimensional world as a bridge between the fourth and fifth dimensions, and ever since I realized that the spirits were the ones responsible for the music that was coming out of me, I've dedicated my life to doing what they want me to do. The ones who are on my side, the ones who are my friends, and also for a long time I had to dedicate myself to fighting the ones who weren't my friends, which I don't have to do any more because I've got friendly spirits protecting me now."

In April 1998 Dave Navarro parted ways amicably with the Chili Peppers, with all parties agreeing that it would be the best move. In a selfless last effort, Navarro told his soon-to-be ex-bandmates that the one guitarist they most needed was none other than Frusciante. This resonated with everyone concerned and Flea contacted the recovering guitarist to see if he would be interested. John jumped at the chance, with the first rehearsal going well despite his wasted figure and lack of chops on his instrument.

"It was great," he said later, "but I had very little technical skill. I'd hardly played guitar for five years; I'd mostly been painting. But the way they took me back made me feel good about myself. I had very little ability, but it didn't matter to them, it was just the spirit of what I was doing and the fact that it was me. It felt so good to have friends who really believed in me when nobody else did, because I was a person who people pretty much thought of as finished... I'm so tuned into these imaginary realms of existence that they're the places I'm writing about when I write lyrics. I've had so many visions of other lives and what it's like in other dimensions, I can write about them with clarity and focus."

Asked if he was finding it difficult to withdraw from the enormous heroin and cocaine addictions that had almost consumed him, he said, "I don't battle against it. If anything it helps me. I have no temptation whatsoever to do drugs, but the experience was beneficial to me. Not to say that I'd see drugs as beneficial for anybody else. I know a lot of people who took drugs and it destroyed every one of them. It destroyed me too, but I managed to pull myself back and benefit from the whole thing. It's a sure-fire way to fuck up your whole life, but what I felt on them and what I learned from them I'll never turn my back on. I wouldn't trade the experience for anything. I'm very proud of the life I've lived. I'm very proud of who I am and where I've been."

Was he enjoying life again? Remarkably, so it seemed. "I'm very happy. Every day I tell myself that I love life so much... I'm at peace with myself. I think that when I was a young, confused and stupid person who actually hadn't lived much, I think I really wanted to be who I am now. In a way I'm proud of my experiences because they've helped me get here."

Frusciante retained an unorthodox, but somehow appealing, take on life—and death: "I like death a lot. It comes up a lot, it's always been in my songs, especially in the last few years, since I've really come to terms with all the confusing thoughts that I've had my whole life about the subject. And through the five years that I wasn't a part of the world, I resolved a lot of my thoughts on the subject, and I saw a lot of things really clearly—clearly enough where for me, there is no doubt about that subject and I have no questions about that subject. A lot of people sit around and think 'I wonder what happens after I die' or 'I wonder if there is a heaven' or something, or 'I wonder, do we live on,' questions like that. I don't think about any questions like that, everything is straight in my head. I write songs because that's the only way I can express what I've learned. I can't express it by talking about it in an interview or writing a book about it, at least not while I'm alive, so for me, the best way for me to get it across to people is to write songs which, in a lot of ways, are abstract, but to me, that's... in a lot of ways, death is very abstract. The way our brains work on earth, death is a really... compared to the equivalent of our brains after we die is very abstract, and there's a lot of abstractness to get used to.

"For people who pay attention to the lyrics of people like Captain Beefheart and Syd Barrett, people like that have a good head-start on death. I suppose, in my lyrics, it's a combination of being inspired by those abstractly oriented lyricists that, to me, seem like the most meaningful words that anyone has put to music. It's a combination between that and, to me, what are very concrete things that I've seen for myself about that subject. But it's important to understand that when I'm talking about death, I'm not talking about ceasing to exist or something—that's very uninteresting to me. If that was my philosophy, I definitely wouldn't think it was important enough to put it into songs. For me, death is a new way of seeing things, and for me death is a new reality. For me, there is an endless amount of things I could write about that. I will write songs about death all the way up until I die or as long as I'm writing songs. To me, the songs that I write about that definitely deal with the infinite in that songs that tell stories don't."

The result of all this inner exploration and slightly self-congratulatory analysis was 1999's phenomenal *Californication*, the album that saw the Red Hot Chili Peppers elevated back to the top of the rock tree. A bona fide classic, it went on to sell over 12 million copies—even more than *Blood Sugar Sex Magik*. But many of the Chilis' fanbase were dumbfounded by the album. Far from the rootin'-tootin' hardcore funk that had made their previous albums (with the exception of the ironically lukewarm *One Hot Minute*) so exciting, *Californication* was loaded with ballads and smooth, sweet pop—the logical conclusion of the process that had seen the band abandon their balls-out punk of the 1980s via the warm balladry of "Under The Bridge" and beyond.

The literally rejuvenated Chilis took to the road in the wake of *Californication*, touring extensively with Pearl Jam and the Foo Fighters and headlining Woodstock 99, where sections of the crowd went berserk, spoiling the event with the rioting, vandalism and violence that was Generation X's equivalent to the peace and love vibes of 1969. A guest appearance on Fishbone's *Psychotic Friends Nuttwerx* album followed and the Chilis entered the new millennium as— once again—one of the biggest bands in the world.

After five years in the wilderness, the band were jubilant. Asked how life on the road treated the band in the wake of their recent success, Kiedis enthused, "It's all great. I feel fortunate to have experienced the entire gamut of touring possibilities. A lot of bands stay at the club level, and never get to experience all these other levels, of playing festivals, arenas, stadiums. Other bands become so popular immediately that they never get the pleasure of paying their dues. We've experienced every single level. When we were playing the shit-hole clubs of America we were having so much fun, it was so thrilling to go out there and play for 40 people in Ohio who didn't know what they were in for, and just grab them by the throat with jokes and energy. Now we get to go to Hyde Park and play for 80,000 people three nights in a row. It's a whole different mindset. Now we get on a plane and fly at 3am from Brussels to Edinburgh and stay in exotic hotels. It wouldn't be nearly as interesting, though, if we hadn't experienced all the stepping stones along the way."

Older, wiser, and more able to cope with the rigorous touring schedule that derailed them in the first place, the bandmembers threw themselves into more recording sessions, hoping to outdo even the mighty *Californication*. "The old magic is back," Flea enthused. "Everything is possible and that's a great feeling. We've grown as people and musicians. So, the music is different. It's a different time, but it's still great, even better than it was. We're jamming and that works really well. We don't talk much about songs or how songs should be constructed. We just start to play and see what happens, how they develop. We improvise a lot. We find a groove. We experiment and somehow it turns into music."

Much of this newfound joy was down to Frusciante, Flea explained. "With Dave [Navarro], it wasn't possible to work like this. With him it was more like a long thought process, endless discussions, and it took a long time. We talked about what riff should be played and all that. With John it's completely different. We just play. I don't mean to diss Dave in any way. He is a great person and he's a great guitarist, but the way we work is just different. You never know why it happens with some people and not with others. It's pointless. It's like asking why you fall in love. There is no real reason, nothing that can be explained or that would make sense."

Flea and the others were in awe of what Frusciante had been through, with the bass player telling the press, "You just don't do what John did—and live." John himself, now with a new set of shiny dentures, glossy hair and only the terrible ruins of his arms ("It's actually more from coke than from heroin," he said. "Coke you're shooting every five minutes. That's what did it to me.") bearing witness to his trials, was humble about his role, expounding only on his desire to embrace more music. "I spent a lot of time after the last tour furthering my understanding of chord theory and learning Beatles and Charles Mingus and Burt Bacharach songs. But I've got a lot more to learn." Asked by *Spin* if all this theory might spoil his muse, he laughed. "Absolutely not. It just leads to making music with a wider variety of emotion. It makes me see even more how infinite music is."

His later influences came from unexpected directions, as he revealed: "People like Jimmy Page and Jimi Hendrix have pretty much been my gods the whole time I was playing. I also like Eddie Van Halen's early guitar playing. But I don't feel like guitar playing went any further after that—not in that technical or flashy direction. And I don't feel like guitar players have started coming at it from a new angle. So I began drawing inspiration from synthesizer players— programmed music, starting with Kraftwerk. It's another way of approaching melodies that guitar players don't really do. For the whole time we were touring for *Californication*, I was practising guitar by playing along with electronic music."

Jazz and its subgenres were still inspiring him, just as they had in the *Blood Sugar Sex Magik* days, he said. "I learned a lot, throughout the making of [*Californication*], from studying Charles Mingus. Learning his chord progressions. I studied a lot of music books, and learned about the way different people construct chord progressions. The Beatles, Burt Bacharach... just things that I'd never have been able to figure out by ear. It started changing the way that I play guitar. Johnny Marr [of The Smiths] was also a big inspiration in just starting to think about the guitar differently."

Thinking about his instrument differently even meant abandoning it for a while. "I don't play guitar unless I'm on stage," he added. "I play clarinet now. I'm much more serious about it than the guitar, to be honest. Right now I'm trying to figure out how to put the notes together, and how to make them wide and deep. I try not to make conscious decisions on either instrument—I just play. Every time I pick up an instrument, I don't know what's going to happen."

Drummer Chad Smith also made much of his desire to gel within the band, laughing: 'I did this session with an old blues guy about two months ago and he said, if I can hear you, you're playing too much. I think he meant if I hear you, you're playing too busy. You know, just make it feel good, man. And it's kind of my mentality with where we're at now. We're just trying to make the best songs we can   I don't feel reined-in or restricted in any way. This album is just a snapshot of where we are right now. It seems like we're in a really good, creative place. We can appreciate the four of us together, the important chemistry. With John coming back, it's amazing. He's an incredible, inspiring person to be around. He's a musician and an artist and he'd come to rehearsal and show up ready. John would have the record written in half an hour. And I think it brought everybody up a level."

Flea too had evidently learned to enjoy the band and his part of it more easily over the years. "Standing in one place and playing isn't what the Red Hot Chili Peppers are about," he smiled. "It's about being the wildest rock band on earth. People buy tickets to see us play, and I'm into entertaining them. I think as much about dancing and being bizarre as I do about playing well. I'm not saying that to do a good show you have to jump around and do an avant-garde dance while spinning on your head—but no one would have liked Charlie Chaplin if he hadn't fallen on his face every once in a while!"

And this happened while he still has the hunger to improve himself, too, as he explained: "The thing that's changed me even more recently is having realized the importance of becoming a loving person: someone who thinks, what can I give, rather than, what am I going to get?

Right now, I'm very eager to learn; I haven't had that feeling for quite a while. I've had that hunger for music as a whole, but not for the bass as an instrument. After we play a gig nowadays, I go back to my hotel room and play even more. I'm trying to figure out new sounds and get my hands and mind to be co-ordinated in a beautiful, flowing way. My dynamic has changed—I really want to improve as a bass player... I'm jamming on grooves and bass lines and trying to find new ones. Also, I'm going to start learning stuff off records to get new perspectives, which is something I've rarely done. I've always played by improvising with myself."

Success, too, has become just another facet of life as a Red Hot Chili Pepper that needs to be managed—and he can do it, as he said. "I don't need to prove anything to anybody," he explained, adding, "I'm secure in myself. But being this popular now, it upsets me to be perceived in a way that I don't want to be perceived—as a misogynist or homophobic or unsympathetic to other people. I have to be more careful not to say things that are misunderstood. Yet I don't feel any different than the way I did when we started this band ten years ago... Sure, I've learned and grown, a lot of things have happened to me. But I think I've always been a kindhearted person. Just because I come and out and go: 'Waaaaagh! Fuck you!' I was into punk rock, man. That's part of what punk rock was about to me—never having to say you're sorry."

Much of *Blood Sugar Sex Magik*'s elegant simplicity comes from Flea's expertise at, and insistence on, a simple, jammed, live approach to songwriting—which translated so well in the event of recording and is what makes the record sound so fresh today. Of the album, he recalled: "I remember trying to play very simply. In the past, I've played some things just to be a bitchin' player, but that wasn't the overall attitude this time around. Jamming well has a lot to do with your understanding of humanity. It also takes hard work and dedication. I think we had been stagnating; getting together in that kind of environment loosened things up."

Extended touring had helped him as a musician, he added. "Touring saps me physically, but not musically. You don't usually realize when it's happening, but the road makes you a better musician, and much more accustomed to playing all the time and thinking on your feet... I found myself playing these simple, elegant bass lines. It was surprising. I just built a rehearsal studio in my house. I can't wait to get back and just jam when I want to—it's been a dream of mine."

The philosophy behind this approach lent weight to his words when he considered his daughter's possible future as a musician. "My only advice [to Clara] is to do whatever you want as long as you don't hurt yourself or anybody else. I would hope she would have the love and self-esteem to make her craft interesting and do something beautiful. In general, I believe that if you don't really love what you're doing, you should stop right away. If you do truly want to play, then you should play your own way and play what makes you feel good. Try to recognize the parts of your character that are your own, because a lot of people do things they think other people will like instead of embracing what they love. Do that on your instrument. Play something you like, not something you'd do for someone else. That's what makes great music."

Of his daughter's budding musical talent, he enthused: "Clara's already a great drummer. I realized it for the first time while we were in London recently... and she got up behind the drum set and started playing boom, pop, boom boom, pop, and I was like, where did that come from? I started playing along with her, and she was right on the groove! I have a drum kit at home, but now I might get her a little set of her own."

Punk rock and its attendant release remains an important outlet for Flea to this day, as he revealed: "One night I put on X's [1980 album] *Los Angeles* really loud, and I just had a total epiphany about why I wanted to play rock music in the first place. I started jumping around and threw my plate against the wall! I was smashing shit. My daughter was like, 'Papa! What's the matter with you?' I threw myself on the ground. I was on the verge of tears, but also of ecstasy." This aggression is evident on the songs on which he has guested, and one of these in particular—Alanis Morissette's 1995 hit "You Oughta Know", on which he and Frusciante's successor Dave Navarro added a certain rock edge. "It was very instinctive!" laughed Flea. "I showed up, rocked out, and split. When I first heard the track, it had a different bassist and guitarist on it; I listened to the bass line and thought, that's some weak shit! It was no flash and no smash! But the vocal was strong, so I just tried to play something good...

"I also played on 'Bust A Move' by Young MC, which was a No. 1 hit. I have a bitter taste in my mouth about that, though, because I feel as though I got ripped off. The bass-line I wrote ended up being a major melody of the tune, and I felt I deserved songwriting credit and money because it was a No. 1 hit. They sold millions of records, and I got $200! My lawyer told them, 'You should throw down Flea some cash,' but the record company said, 'We told him exactly what to play.' No one was even in the room at the time but me and the engineer! It was ridiculous, but I learned from it."

Flea had also played—with a diametrically opposed style—on an album of traditional North African music by a singer called Cheikha Rimitti entitled *Sidi Mansour*. Of the rather obscure album, he enthused, "She sings so beautifully. It's rhyme and traditional North African music mixed with me on bass, Robert Fripp on guitar, and the Dead Kennedys' East Bay Ray on guitar. The songs are kind of tribalish grooves. I'm playing funky bass over percussion and microtonal flute."

One day, he has promised, he will record a solo album. "It won't be a solo bass record; the bass will just play the bass lines in the songs. I'm not saying the melody can't be featured on the bass, but I think if a song is about the bass guitar, it'll revolve around a beautiful line with things layered on top of it—kind of a sexy dub type of thing. I'm also going to make a record with my friend John Lurie, who's the sax player from the Lounge Lizards."

Asked if there were still other artists with whom he wanted to play bass, he responded with enthusiasm. "Everybody!" he said. "I play with Steven Perkins [Jane's Addiction/Porno For Pyros drummer]. I just finished working on Roger Waters' new record. I even got a call from Jeff Beck's people. They asked me if I wanted to work on his new album. I was really into it, but then I found out that he's going into the studio the day we go back on the road. I had to say no... I really think I could light a fire under his ass. It's not that he's an old fart or anything, I just think I could really shake things up."

As for the way he viewed the Red Hot Chili Peppers, it's clear that as a bandmember and as a songwriter he felt much affection and optimism for their future: "Both individually and as a band, we are growing and changing and finding new ways to express ourselves... Our lives are different, because we are different people every day and are always writing and changing and arriving in different places. When I play songs that we wrote ten years ago, I respect them for what they are; I honor them and pour my heart and my body into every note—but for me to not change and grow with it would be stale and uninteresting... Everything that I've ever done is part of who I am. I love playing all the ways that I can play... I just want to keep changing and growing as a musician."

But this is Flea—the firebrand punk bass thing—and to this day he retains much of the madman character that made *Blood Sugar Sex Magik* so entertaining—new, stripped-down, selfless bass approach or not. As he said a couple of years later of his *One Hot Minute* song "Pea", which contained the line "Homophobic redneck dick" (causing a new "clean" version of the album to be recut for the benefit of the giant retailer Wal-Mart): "I did get some shit for it, but fuck those people!... I mean, if someone says, 'I'm not going to buy your record, but I'll buy these songs', then OK—buy those songs. I'd rather they hear it all, but to hell with my ego...".

After the enormous success of *Blood Sugar Sex Magik*, life was different for all the players involved—even Rick Rubin. Most notably, he moved largely away from hip-hop (he told one interviewer: "I haven't heard anything in rap [recently] to make me excited enough to be involved in it") and into more esoteric forms of rock. The high point of the 1990s for him, after the Chili Peppers, would probably have been his Grammy-winning work with the late country star Johnny Cash, with whom he worked after the label split was complete. As he recalled, "I felt like between Def Jam and American, I had only ever really signed new artists, and only really worked with young people on their first albums. It seemed like it would be a fun challenge to work with an established artist. I tried to think, 'Who's a great artist, who's a legendary artist, who's maybe not in the best place, or not finding the support they need to do their best work.' Johnny was the first person I thought of."

A relationship grew—with Rubin's artist-relations skills presumably heightened further by his dealings with the friendly, if damaged, Chili Peppers: "I liked [Cash] very much. I would say we hit it off, though we didn't say much at our first meeting. We were both pretty quiet. But it felt strong, and it felt like there was potential for really good work to be done. I think he was almost at the point of giving up. I think he'd probably made a hundred albums, and making an album wasn't a big deal to him. It wasn't important to him. It was just another one: 'Eighteen months roll by, put out another one, doesn't really matter, no one really cares.'

"I think that's where he was at, where the record-making part of his artistry didn't matter so much to him after being not treated so well, after being dropped from Columbia, his longtime label, and then being at Mercury, where he was not really cared for very much. I think he may have still been going through the motions, but I don't think he was emotionally invested in the record-making process. I think the idea of doing something new appealed to him, but I don't think it was that big of a deal. Until we started having some success, I don't know that he cared that much about his recording career, again, only because of the way he had been treated. It was almost beaten out of him in some way."

How he had approached working with Cash was a different ballgame to that of the resolutely upbeat Chili Peppers: "I guess I thought of the legendary image of the Man In Black, and thought that we could find material, or write material, and kind of use that imagery as a framework for the kind of songs that we were going to do. Make sure that whatever he sang suited the mythic character, that was really maybe a caricature of himself. There was probably some of him in it. That's probably where it came from.

"But we were trying to find, from a content point of view, what someone who loved what Johnny Cash was would want to hear him sing. Sometimes we would pick songs that you wouldn't think of him singing, like a Beck song, something you wouldn't think a Johnny Cash fan would want, or a Soundgarden song. But it's less where it came from, and more the actual content of the material. I always tried to pick material that really suited him, that when you heard him singing the words, it made sense, and you feel it. You feel the truth in what he's singing, whether you wrote the song or not."

In the late 1990s Rubin hooked up with the fascinating, unpredictable American-Armenian rock band System Of A Down, who enjoyed a string of leftfield hits. Of the band's fourth studio album (in production at the time of writing), Rubin nodded: "System's awesome. I saw them in rehearsal the other day, working on their new stuff. It's going to be a whole new re-invention". He also worked with Audioslave, the new project of ex-Rage Against The Machine members Tom Morello, Tim Commerford, and Brad Wilk and sometime Soundgarden singer Chris Cornell. Of their second album, Rubin pondered: "I'm really excited about that one because the last Audioslave album was more of a studio project. They'd never even done one show, so in some ways they weren't really a band. Now they've done lots of touring, and I feel like the potential is so much greater to do a really powerful album, better than the first one."

As he looked back on his career, he mused, "I kind of started where I am; I'm really just doing the same things I've always done. I didn't come up through the business. I've never been an engineer, I've never worked in a studio, I've never done the things that a lot of people have done to become producers. I started as a producer, I'm still a producer. And I've always, from the beginning, run a record company. The first records I made were on my label. I've worked with other labels along the way as an independent producer, like for Red Hot Chili Peppers for Warner Brothers. But I also produce for my company, and then I'm more involved, like with Johnny Cash and System Of A Down...

"It's always been that way, so it's hard for me to judge what I do versus what other people do. Because I don't know what other producers do. I know a lot of producers were engineers who graduated to being producers, but I can't imagine what qualifications an engineer would have to be a producer. To me, it's just a different job, but there are some great engineers who become great producers. Again, I don't know what they do. I only kind of know what I do. and I'm not too sure of that!"

At the time of writing in spring 2005, Rubin sits, guru-like, at the top of the rock production tree, and is among the world's most credible producers. He retains a healthy degree of self-deprecation, saying of his time at Def Jam, "If I would have stayed, it would have been completely different. I don't know if it would have been the same successful thing that it is. I can't imagine what it would have been like, had I stayed, because I didn't. I mean, Guns N' Roses asked me to produce their first album, and I didn't do it. When it had all that success, people asked me if I was sad that I didn't do it. It's like, 'I don't know that it wouldn't have been the same thing that it was. No one might have cared".

Once again, Rubin was at the helm of the Chilis new album, titled *By The Way*, and it was his influence that would help make it such a hit. Although Frusciante—now, it seemed, the creative leader behind the music—had had his own ideas in mind for the record ("I wanted this album to have more dimension, more different sounds and more movements in the chord progressions. But I also wanted it to be more fun"), it was Rubin's vintage obsessions which had added the flavour. "Rick Rubin and I would get together every day," Frusciante reported, "and he's got these CDs of AM radio hits from the 1960s. And they'd have stuff by the The Mamas And The Papas and songs like 'Cherish' by the Association and 'Georgie Girl' [by The Seekers]. All those songs are all about harmonies. I've been practicing harmonizing a lot in the past year and a half. My friend Josh and I would sit around and sing Beatles songs, or that Velvet Underground song, "Jesus", which has a harmony in it. Anything we could think of that had harmony."

These pop elements had led to a subtler guitar sound from Frusciante, as he explained. "I played with a much cleaner guitar sound on this record; I don't have that many reasons to play dirty any more. When you want to play heavy, you got to play dirty, but the clean sound is the natural sound. Personally, my favorite guitar sound is straight into a four track—straight into the board."

By The Way appeared in 2002 and was the expected successor to Californication, providing a handful of melodic hits and bringing the band even more fans. Just as he had on Blood Sugar Sex Magik, Kiedis had written a clutch of love songs to Los Angeles, explaining: "[The song] 'By The Way' is about the color of any given night in the Los Angeles basin. What's going on in the streets—from a crime in a parking garage to a sexy little girl named Annie singing songs to some guy who she's got a crush on. It's an atmospheric lyric. Just painting a picture rather than a whole plot. The feeling that inspired the chorus melody is one of waiting, hoping and wanting to make a connection with another person. A romantic connection. Just that feeling of, 'is this gonna be the night?'... In very obscure, less than obvious ways, I feel a lot of it is about either being in love or the desire to be in love. It's definitely what I've been feeling for the last year. A profound sense of wanting love in my daily experience... I love being associated with LA because it is such a paradox of a land. And I believe in paradox as being a kind of higher truth. LA is the most ridiculous place in the world, but it's also the greatest place in the world."

At the end of the line, Kiedis viewed the future with a serene eye, both in terms of his health and his future as a band member. "My chemistry is in great shape these days, so it happens naturally. When I listen to music, when I look at the sky, when I'm with my friends, when I sleep with my dog, when I swim, run, or ride my Vespa down the hill. I don't have to release [body chemicals] all at once any more; I can take them as they're doled out by nature... There is no one that I'd rather play with than the guys I'm playing with. There is nothing that I have to say that I can't say in this band. John, because he doesn't write the lyrics or sing the lead vocals in the Red Hot Chili Peppers, has that voice in him to write lyrics and sing lead vocals, so he has to go make solo records, because it's in him. He would be insane not to. If, God forbid, this dissolved, then I would have to find a solo avenue. But I'm not going to find better people to play with."

And so the Red Hot Chili Peppers rose again to the top of the music world. A fully evolved sociocultural phenomenon, they had even spawned charity projects such as Flea's Silverlake Conservatory Of Music in East Hollywood, a foundation the bass player had established to provide local residents with affordable music lessons. "The fact that people can stay sincere and have joy in their lives in the face of phoniness or economic elitism is a testament to the spirit of Los Angeles," explained Flea. "Whether it be street kids from broken homes like me and Anthony, or victims of huge racism like the black community, or the Mexican community, crawling across the border just to survive. There are pockets where all these people come together and live in a creative and vibrant atmosphere, and that's the Los Angeles I love."

In an almost metaphorical aside—he could have been talking about his band, or the city, or the conservatory—he said: "The thing that survives has to be really beautiful, and have a really substantial core to it. And it has to be determined to stick to its guns and do what it's gonna do."

As Kiedis told *Playboy*, "Our ambition is to create beauty rather than to fight ugliness. We would rather try to make people happy than to try and stop them from being sad."

John Frusciante—the tortured genius who survived fame and near-oblivion, returning to lead his band to the very top, said it all: "There is a weird chemistry between us. The way I play guitar, it only works when Flea is the bassist, and Flea can only write songs the way he does when Anthony sings. In a way we're all co-dependent and we know it, but we also trust each other. It is a second chance for all of us."

the influence

What happened to music after the
Red Hot Chili Peppers made *Blood Sugar Sex Magik*

After the dust settled on the rock scene in the wake of *Blood Sugar Sex Magik*, the world's music fans could gain a little perspective on the impact it had made. Above the tumultuous musical activity by acts big and small, an overarching pantheon of supergiant stadium bands stood—which itself was undergoing some seismic changes.

The biggest heavy-rock bands in the world in the previous year—1990—were Bon Jovi and Aerosmith, both of which had evolved by this stage into anodyne acts who had produced albums full of safe, anthemic music for several years. However, the following year both were replaced by much heavier, darker acts from the previously more niche realm of heavy metal: Metallica and Guns N' Roses. In August 1991 Metallica released their fifth, self-titled studio album, a ponderous but radio-friendly behemoth that introduced a whole generation of previously metal-illiterate music fans to the joys of the riff and the moshpit thanks to its hummable, air-guitarable riffs and song structures. Metallica themselves had undergone something of a style change during the recording of the album, moving from fast, progressive thrash metal featuring many tempo and riff changes to a simpler, more digestible style that propelled *Metallica* (the "Black Album") to eventual sales of 20 million and beyond. Established fans stood and stared as "their" metal band hit the charts—but with the benefit of hindsight we can see that the fertile mood of change that enveloped the music scene at the time made such a development not only possible but probable.

As for Guns N' Roses, their rise to global dominance was a story even more improbable than that of Metallica. A highly unstable five-piece supported, it seemed, only by booze and narcotics, GNR had recorded their much-worshipped debut album, *Appetite For Destruction*, in 1988 and toured incessantly, scoring radio airplay along the way with a series of timeless singles including "Paradise City" and "Sweet Child O' Mine". Led by the mercurial singer W. Axl Rose, the band's hubris reached its logical level in 1991 when they released two double albums on the same day, entitled *Use Your Illusion I* and *II*. This over-the-top move had attracted an enormous fanbase—and Metallica and GNR realized that a double-headline tour with both bands would be mutually beneficial. Taking the Chili Peppers-influenced Faith No More along as support, the bands toured the planet, making 1991 and 1992 their own.

But for the first time, the biggest two bands in the world would have rivals—less commercially successful, for sure, but in terms of musical inventiveness and sheer cool, not in the same league. In 1991 these pioneering groups were Nirvana and the Red Hot Chili Peppers.

Of the former, much has been said, with the grunge wave they rode a brief but bright flash of activity. A whole raft of grunge, grunge-influenced and post-grunge bands followed in Nirvana's wake, including major acts in their own right such as Pearl Jam, Soundgarden, the Screaming Trees, the

Smashing Pumpkins, and Hole. However, the initial impetus of the movement had already stalled by the time Nirvana singer Kurt Cobain killed himself in April 1994, with the generic "alternative rock" tag a more enduring label—applied to any act with a raw (grunge-influenced) sound or a funky (Chilis-influenced) edge.

Although the limiting—and badly dated—but useful terms "rap-metal" and "funk-metal" had been a popular critic's idiom since Faith No More's breakthrough single of January 1990 ("Epic", which had been a worldwide hit), both of them came into play more widely in the wake of *Blood Sugar Sex Magik*. A whole host of bands—genuinely or otherwise funky, but almost all categorised by a bass player who slapped and popped on his instrument—came to prominence in America and Europe, including 24-7 Spyz, Catfish, Fishbone, Guano Apes, Infectious Grooves, Primus, Living Colour, Madball, Mr. Bungle, Rage Against The Machine, and Shootyz Groove. All of these acts owed at least some aspect of their style to the Red Hot Chili Peppers and their breakthrough album. The rock scene had come to recognize funk—and through it, racial diversity (as many of the players were black)—meaning that the impact of this one album had social as well as cultural consequences.

Not that the Chilis themselves were overly concerned with all this at the time. Asked if he felt much kinship with either the grunge acts or the alternative funk-metal bands, Kiedis shrugged. "No, because what they do has nothing to do with what we do. That particular clique of [grunge] bands are all from the same city [Seattle], and all came to the attention of the music-consuming public at approximately the same time. We've been running our own steady course of affairs, exclusive to anything that they've done. So there really isn't a pocket of other bands that we sort of gauge ourselves by." If anything, the wave of new bands had defocused the relationship the Chilis once had with their fellow Los Angeles musicians. "There was a time when Fishbone and Jane's Addiction were on the move, and there were even bands before that like The Minutemen that we felt a lot of kinship with," he added. 'But not any more. After Jane's Addiction and The Minutemen dissolved, that feeling of being connected because we were from the same city went the same way."

"Now all the bands that wanted to be Guns N' Roses or U2 want to be Nirvana," Flea added. "As soon as someone says, OK, alternative rock is big and that's the thing that makes all the money now, then it eats itself alive."

By 1996 the rap-metal and funk-metal terms had been largely discarded in favor of the catch-all term "nu-metal" (initially "new metal"). A now-outdated term encompassing the hip-hop-influenced music of Korn, the art-metal of Tool, and a couple of years later the furious DJ-assisted riffage of Slipknot and Limp Bizkit, nu-metal wasn't easy to define—but it grew enormously, attracting a vast base of listeners by the end of the decade. The Red Hot Chili Peppers watched in disdainful awe as the music they had helped to create—by injecting a dose of funk into the tamely vanilla rock mainstream—threatened to consume the world.

"There's all this angry, screaming metal now," marvelled Flea. "It's part of a thing that we started, in a lot of ways. This funky sound with rapping and guitars has been turned into something very boring: right-wing, redneck bullshit. It was always funny to me, the way the Chili Peppers were perceived as this macho-jock thing. We took off our shirts a lot, and Anthony wrote a lot of songs about sex. But I feel like the music is frequently feminine. I've always been, like, the girly-boy. I'm just a sensitive little fuck, you know?"

Kiedis was equally uncomplimentary. "I don't think any of those conservative, ultra-aggro, rap-metal bands had the funk influence or punk rock energy that we had," he said with uncharacteristic vehemence. "Even when I was 14, I didn't have such one-dimensional angst."

But the usually perceptive Kiedis wasn't quite on the money with this last comment. Although many of the nu-metallers—mainly B-league acts such as Insolence and Spineshank—didn't really transcend their shouty roots and were indeed too one-sided to last long, the bigger and more talented acts soon outgrew the big shorts, big mouth, big aggression recipe and moved on. The founding fathers of the alt.metal movement had been too multifaceted for that not to happen.

So who were these talented, influential bands that spawned a whole new movement? The Red Hot Chili Peppers were the godfathers of the rap/funk/metal template, based on their equal love of punk, funk, and metal: but other, equally influential bands helped out, too.

The most obvious of these is Faith No More, whose bass player Bill Gould knew his way around a slapping fretboard. He was never as lightning-fingered as Flea—but then so few modern players are—only Robert Trujillo (Suicidal Tendencies, Infectious Grooves, Ozzy Osbourne, Metallica) and Les Claypool (Primus, Sausage) come near him. But Gould propelled FNM along through several albums of raw funked-up metal, with his later work as alternative as any other of the era.

A San Francisco Bay area band consisting initially of Gould, drummer Mike "Puffy" Bordin, keyboard player Wade Worthington, and guitarist Mark Bowen, Faith No More started life in 1981 as Faith No Man. After recruiting various temporary singers including future Hole frontwoman Courtney Love, the band ended up with Chuck Mosely and the line-up settled down when Bowen was replaced by "Big" Jim Martin. The band adapted its name to Faith No More and Worthington was replaced by the bizarrely named Roddy Bottum, soon to come out as one of the 1990s' first gay rock stars.

Like the Chilis, Faith No More paid their dues before they hit the big time. A four-song demo led to a deal with the independent Mordam label and an album, *We Care A Lot*, was issued in 1985. The title track combined Gould's percussive slap-bass with Martin's heavy riffs, and can be seen as one of the very first funk-metal songs. FNM then moved to another company, Slash, which released *Introduce Yourself* in 1987. Epic ballads such as "Annie's Song" and mellow strumathons such as "The Crab Song" combined with the harder material to make it a real classic. A world tour followed, but Mosely had fallen out with the others and was ousted when the band got home in January 1989. The crucial move that propelled FNM to stardom came when vocalist Mike Patton, of Californian easy-listening/metal band Mr. Bungle, took Mosely's place. An animated performer with an impressive vocal range, Patton inspired the band to far greater efforts.

The resulting album, *The Real Thing*, was a career landmark, with riffs aplenty courtesy of the eccentric Martin, Patton's spiraling harmonies and sinister whispers, and the expert textures of Gould, Bottum, and Bordin making it an eye-opener for fans unused to this new, varied approach to metal. At around this stage, a public slanging match erupted between Patton and Anthony Kiedis: the two bands had been endlessly compared (Kiedis had spoken of his fear that FNM would be regarded as the instigators of the punk-funk style, when chronologically speaking, the Peppers were way ahead), although with the emergence of *Blood Sugar Sex Magik* and *Angel Dust* it became apparent how different the bands were. In any case, the enormous sales of the former made any comparison academic: while FNM were worshipped, they were unable to play at stadium level (other than as guests on the aforementioned Metallica/Guns N' Roses tour of 1992) whereas the Chilis made those very venues their domain.

Angel Dust marked the peak of FNM's commercial fortunes and stayed near the top of the charts for months, helped along by the excellent singles "Midlife Crisis", "A Small Victory", "Everything's Ruined", and a cover of the Commodores' "Easy", a surprise No. 1 that led to a reissue of *Angel Dust*. However, the rot was setting in a little and the disillusioned Jim Martin departed in November 1993—he now grows pumpkins on his own farm in the Mid-West. He was replaced by Mr. Bungle axeman Trey Spruance on the next album, 1995's *King For A Day, Fool For A Lifetime*, but the moment had passed and the album didn't sell well outside the FNM hardcore fanbase. Spruance himself didn't last long and his place was taken by Duh guitarist Dean Menta.

As the Chilis themselves found to their cost, the mid to late 1990s weren't kind to the bands which had been so influential to the alternative rock scene, and despite well-received solo projects from Bottum (Imperial Teen) and Patton (Mr. Bungle), 1997's coyly-titled *Album Of The Year* proved to be Faith No More's last. In April 1998 Gould released the following message: "After 15 long and fruitful years, Faith No More have decided to put an end to speculation regarding their imminent break-up... by breaking up. The decision among the members is mutual, and there will be no pointing of fingers, no naming of names, other than stating, for the record, that 'Puffy started it'. Furthermore, the split will now enable each member to pursue his individual project(s) unhindered. Lastly, and most importantly, the band would like to thank all of those fans and associates that have stuck with and supported the band throughout its history."

The fans were dismayed, but accepted that Faith No More's relevance in the era of nu-metal was questionable, although their pioneering status is evident. Patton has gone on to form Fantomas and Tomahawk and launch a record label, Ipecac, while the others are still making music in some capacity or other. FNM are constantly asked about a possible reformation, just as the Chilis would have been in the alternate future that would have opened up had they split in the wake of the unloved *One Hot Minute*. Despite their rivalry, the stories of the two bands are similar, sharing punk roots, musical changes of direction, and the departure of their charismatic guitarist leading to career doldrums.

The same career links can't be derived of the career of another successful alternative rock and rap-rock-influencing band, The Beastie Boys—other, that is, than the significant fact that they have been guided by Rick Rubin almost every step of the way. But the Beasties did their share of influencing, pilfering rock sounds, funking them up, adding a hip-hop backing track, and turning into globally successful stars. Like less credible contemporaries such as Vanilla Ice and much more admired successors such as Eminem—plus a host of white-boy rappers in the 1990s and Noughties—the fact that the Beasties were Caucasian meant that hip-hop aficionados were initially unconvinced of their abilities. Add to this the bandmembers' middle-class backgrounds and it's little wonder that few listeners took them seriously on their appearance in 1983, when they abandoned their early hardcore punk roots on a comedy rap single, "Cookie Puss".

Ironically, as a punk band the Beastie Boys had enjoyed much more credibility. Initially consisting of vocalist Mike D (Michael Diamond), guitarist John Berry, bassist MCA (Adam Yauch), and drummer Kate Schellenbach (later to return in the band Luscious Jackson), the band had formed in Manhattan in 1981. Demonstrating their Black Flag influences on the *Pollywog Stew* EP, released by the local Ratcage label, the group scored support slots with The Misfits but were hampered by the early departure of Berry and Schellenbach. The punk roots the band later cherished were almost exactly those of the Chili Peppers, apart from the fact that the bands were on opposite sides of America—and infused just as much with the spirit of their home cities.

The Beasties' move to a rap direction came after the recruitment of Ad-Rock (Adam Horovitz, the son of playwright Israel Horovitz). After the "Cookie Puss" single became a surprise club hit, the trio hooked up with New York student Rick Rubin, who was looking for bands to sign to his new label, Def Jam. A second single, the feebly-titled "Rock Hard", flopped, but the follow-up, the riotous "She's On It" (based on an AC/DC sample), was a genuine sensation, leading to a tour with Madonna. A jaunt with Run-DMC helped matters along further, and all this exposure led to a deal with Columbia, who released the Rubin-produced *Licensed To Ill* in 1986.

A global hit, *Licensed To Ill* went platinum in two months and was the fastest-selling debut album in Columbia's history. A barrage of juvenile sexual references, primitive rhymes, and semi-hardcore riffing, the record touched a nerve in teenage listeners worldwide. A touch of controversy was caused by the frat-boy sexism of songs like "Girls", which helped sales along nicely, as well as the eye-opening cover art, which depicted a crashed plane. The Beasties' penchant for wearing Volkswagen badges on necklaces led to a feeding-frenzy of attacks on Golfs and Polos worldwide, leading many an enraged VW owner to wire his car up to the electricity supply as a deterrent to thieves.

Like the Chilis, the Beastie Boys endured serious critical flak for any style change. All the teenage hysteria—plus the Beastie Boys' live show, which featured semi-naked girls writhing in cages—meant that the follow-up album, *Paul's Boutique*, shocked many fans with its serious, almost obscure sounds and general air of maturity. The band had enlisted the help of the Dust Brothers production duo, who had laced the album with psychedelic samples, much to the bemusement of the rap fans who had expected more simple riffs and toilet humor. *Paul's Boutique* failed to match its predecessor's success—although the revisionist view is now that it was a seminal album, leading to the success of Beck and other professional obscurists—and many observers consigned the Beastie Boys to career oblivion.

As the Chilis had done after their first major dose of success, the trio displayed some native cunning and immediately started to operate on a wider level. A record label, Grand Royal, was set up; Horovitz acted in films such as *A Kiss Before Dying*; Diamond founded a clothing line, X-Large; and the band built their own studio. Wisely, the next album, 1992's *Check Your Head*, was a return to the Beasties' punk roots, also utilizing the talents of keyboard player Money Mark. This album marks the second phase of the band's career and the most influential: a deft fusion of rock, punk, funk, and hip-hop, its similarities to *Blood Sugar Sex Magik*—culturally rather than musically—are evident.

Although Kiedis was right when he pointed out that the Beastie Boys made their music by using other people's records, it could also be argued that the similarities in musical style which both sets of musicians' experimental sides provided drew them together. But the fact remains that the Chilis use real guitar, bass, and drums—and that gives them a real edge.

The same strengths apply to the remarkable Jane's Addiction, the band that gave the Chilis their fifth guitarist in the shape of Dave Navarro. They too shaped the alternative-rock world profoundly, with their sexual ambiguities, their splendid artistic pretensions, and their knowingly penetrating take on everything they addressed. Formed in 1984 in Los Angeles, and consisting of ex-Psi Com singer Perry Farrell, guitarist Navarro, bassist Eric Avery, and drummer Stephen Perkins, Jane's Addiction initially scared a few people off with their intense brew of metal, punk and jazz influences. However, those that *did* get the Jane's Addiction bug were fiercely vocal in support of their chosen band, who had released a live album recorded at the Roxy in Hollywood, and a buzz developed rapidly on the LA club scene, leading to a bidding war. This was eventually won by Warners, who released *Nothing's Shocking* in 1988. Slightly controversial in content and cover art, the album spent over six months in the charts and led to the formation of an international fanbase.

Ritual De Lo Habitual was an even more successful record, released two years later, but Farrell felt that the band had run its course and set up a festival, Lollapalooza, to host the band's farewell tour. After the band split in 1991, the Lollapalooza concept refused to die, however, and went on to become an annual fixture for the next few years, showcasing all kinds of new bands—including, of course, the Chilis—and ultimately being supplanted by the various Ozzfests, Tattoo The Earths, Family Values, and Warped tours that sprang up in its wake. Farrell went on to form Porno For Pyros while Navarro joined the Red Hot Chili Peppers—and Jane's Addiction reformed in 2003, much to the pleasure of their large fanbase, many of whom are Chilis fans too. Without Jane's Addiction there would be little art-metal of any kind, as followers of Tool, Orgy, Marilyn Manson, and the other more aesthetically focused acts of their ilk will acknowledge.

By the middle of the Noughties, the alternative rock wave had expanded and broadened to the point where it was too large a term to be truly significant. Mainstream metal had become an interlaced tapestry of "emo" bands like Funeral For A Friend, goth acts such as HIM and Evanescence, and operatic, orchestral acts like Nightwish. Nu-metal had been and gone, reaching critical mass in about 2001 and then disappearing with shocking rapidity.

It was replaced by garage rock, spearheaded by The Strokes, The Hives, The Datsuns, and The White Stripes, and later still by the polished, angular new wave sounds of Franz Ferdinand and others. Only the best of the nu-metal acts survived: of the original pantheon, only Slipknot are really at the top of their game. Limp Bizkit and Korn, once massive sellers, have suffered serious career setbacks; Coal Chamber, Deftones, Glassjaw, Taproot, Papa Roach, and Spineshank are marginalized; Soulfly and Fear Factory have sought a fanbase—with some success—in the extreme metal movement by toughening up their sound; and Linkin Park, once the metal boy band *du jour*, is tinkering with hip-hop. There has also been a notable rise in the popularity of so-called desert rock, with Queens Of The Stone Age leading the pack in a whole new direction (incidentally, QOTSA supported the Chilis in 2004).

Somewhat to one side of all these bands stands the remarkable Marilyn Manson. But this group is as much a rock or a glam band as a metal act, and as such is something of an interesting oddity. Similarly, there is Nine Inch Nails, whose career started before the nu-metal trend had taken off but whose industrial/metal combination was undoubtedly an enormous influence.

But the true influence of the Red Hot Chili Peppers and associated, but lesser, bands lies in the ethos behind the music being made today. No longer do rock, punk, and metal bands have to conform to genre parameters— the strictures that defined their style of music and which were rarely broken before cult late 1980s and early 90s acts such as the Chilis cast them aside to enormous public approval. The sound, the look, the production, and the marketing of the new, more experimental breed of musicians are all geared towards a wider appreciation of what music can be, of what music means, and of what music can bring us all. After all, the doors are open for anyone to work in whichever genre they choose.

Traditional heavy metal bands would have shuddered in the 1970s—and even later—at the mere thought of using drum machines, samples, rapping, and scratching in their songs, but these are now mainstays of dozens of bands. Electronica is also a source of inpiration, with keyboard or computer-sourced sounds, which are harsher or have less groove than hip-hop, leading wherever the user wishes—from mellow ambient sounds to a cortex-shredding barrage of white noise. Let us also not forget the punk versus metal crossover that transformed the early music of the Chilis and led to a whole metalcore movement of bands such as Stampin' Ground, Amen, and other hard-hitting bands.

Together with jazz (the gently atonal chords, noodling solos, and unpredictable chord sequences of the old idiom often crop up in the work of more progressive bands such as Tool and the early Slipknot) and industrial rock (the grinding samples, military beats, harsh textures and intimidating images of industrial may not be for everyone, but followers of Rammstein, Nine Inch Nails and the others would disagree strongly), the heavy music of today is a far different beast than it was before seminal records such as *Blood Sugar Sex Magik*.

Never has such a situation been seen before, and its like will not come again. Revisit *Blood Sugar Sex Magik* with this in mind, and marvel at what it has accomplished.

appendix 1
album discography

The Red Hot Chili Peppers
Release Year: 1984
Label: EMI
Producer: Andrew Gill

Track Listing
1. True Men Don't Kill Coyotes
2. Baby Appeal
3. Buckle Down
4. Get Up And Jump
5. Why Don't You Love Me
6. Green Heaven
7. Mommy Where's Daddy
8. Out In L.A.
9. Police Helicopter
10. You Always Sing
11. Grand Pappy Du Plenty

Freaky Styley
Release Year: 1985
Label: EMI
Producer: George Clinton

Track Listing:
1. Jungle Man
2. Hollywood
3. American Ghost Dance
4. If You Want Me to Stay
5. Nevermind
6. Freaky Styley
7. Blackeyed Blonde
8. The Brothers Cup
9. Battle Ship
10. Lovin' and Touchin'
11. Catholic School Girls Rule
12. Sex Rap
13. Thirty Dirty Birds
14. Yertle the Turtle

Mother's Milk
Release Year: 1989
Label: Capitol
Producer: Michael Beinhorn

Track Listing:
1. Good Time Boys
2. Higher Ground
3. Subway to Venus
4. Magic Johnson
5. Nobody Weird Like Me
6. Knock Me Down
7. Taste the Pain
8. Stone Cold Bush

9. Fire
10. Pretty Little Ditty
11. Punk Rock Classic
12. Sexy Mexican Maid
13. Johnny, Kick a Hole in the Sky

Blood Sugar Sex Magik
Release Year: 1991
Label: Warner Brothers
Producer: Rick Rubin

Track Listing:
1. Power of Equality
2. If You Have To Ask
3. Breaking The Girl
4. Funky Monks
5. Suck My Kiss
6. I Could Have Lied
7. Mellowship Slinky In B Major
8. Righteous and the Wicked, The
9. Give It Away
10. Blood Sugar Sex Magik
11. Under The Bridge
12. Naked In The Rain
13. Apache Rose Peacock
14. Greeting Song
15. My Lovely Man
16. Sir Psycho Sexy
17. They're Red Hot

What Hits!?

[compilation]

Release Year: 1992

Label: Capitol

Track Listing:

1. Higher Ground
2. Fight like A Brave
3. Behind The Sun
4. Me & My Friends
5. Backwoods
6. True Men Don't Kill Coyotes
7. Fire
8. Get Up And Jump
9. Knock Me Down
10. Under The Bridge
11. Show Me Your Soul
12. If You Want Me To Stay
13. Hollywood
14. Jungle Man
15. The Brothers Cup
16. Taste The Pain
17. Catholic School Girls Rule
18. Johnny Kick A Hole In The Sky

Best Of The Red Hot Chili Peppers

[compilation]

Release Year: 1994

Label: EMI

Track Listing:
1. Behind The Sun
2. Johnny Kick A Hole In The Sky
3. Me And My Friends
4. Fire
5. True Men Don't Kill Coyotes
6. Higher Ground
7. Knock Me Down
8. Fight Like A Brave
9. Taste The Pain
10. If You Want Me To Stay

Greatest Hits—10 Best Series
[compilation]
Release Year: 1994
Label: Cema

Track Listing:
1. Behind The Sun
2. Johnny Kick A Hole In The Sky
3. Me And My Friends
4. Fire
5. True Men Don't Kill Coyotes
6. Higher Ground
7. Knock Me Down
8. Fight Like A Brave
9. Taste The Pain
10. If You Want Me To Stay

Out In L.A.
[compilation]
Release Year: 1994
Label: EMI

Track Listing:
1. Higher Ground
2. Hollywood (Africa)(Dance Mix)
3. If You Want Me To Stay (Pink Mustang Mix)
4. Behind The Sun (Ben Gross Remix)
5. Castles Made Of Sand (Live)
6. Special Secret Song Inside (Live)
7. F.U. (Live)
8. Get Up And Jump (Demo)
9. Out In L.A. (Demo)
10. Green Heaven (Demo)
11. Police Helicopter (Demo)
12. Nevermind (Demo)
13. Sex Rap (Demo)
14. Blues For Meister
15. You Always Sing The Same
16. Stranded
17. Flea Fly
18. What It Is
19. Deck The Halls

One Hot Minute
Release Year: 1995
Label: Warner Brothers
Producer: Rick Rubin

Track Listing:
1. Warped
2. Aeroplane
3. Deep Kick
4. My Friends
5. Coffee Shop
6. Pea
7. One Big Mob
8. Walkabout
9. Tearjerker
10. One Hot Minute
11. Falling into Grace
12. Shallow Be Thy Game
13. Transcending

Under The Covers
[compilation]
Release Year: 1998
Label: EMI

Track Listing:
1. They're Red Hot
2. Fire
3. Subterranean Homesick Blues
4. Higher Ground
5. If You Want Me To Stay
6. Why Don't You Love Me
7. Tiny Dancer (Live)
8. Castles Made Of Sand (Live)
9. Dr. Funkenstein (Live)

10. Hollywood (Africa)
11. Search And Destroy
12. Higher Ground (Daddy O Mix)
13. Hollywood (Africa) (Dance Mix)

Californication
Release Year: 1999
Label: Warner Brothers
Producer: Rick Rubin

Track Listing:
1. Around the World
2. Parallel Universe
3. Scar Tissue
4. Otherside
5. Get on Top
6. Californication
7. Easily
8. Porcelain
9. Emitremmus
10. I Like Dirt
11. This Velvet Glove
12. Savior
13. Purple Stain
14. Right on Time
15. Road Trippin'

By The Way
Release Year: 2002
Label: Warner Brothers
Producer: Rick Rubin

Track Listing:
1. By The Way
2. Universally Speaking
3. This Is The Place
4. Dosed
5. Don't Forget Me
6. The Zephyr Song
7. Can't Stop
8. I Could Die For You
9. Midnight
10. Throw Away Your Television
11. Cabron
12. Tear
13. On Mercury
14. Minor Thing
15. Warm Tape
16. Venice Queen

Greatest Hits
[compilation]
Release Year: 2003
Label: Warner Brothers

Track Listing:
1. Under The Bridge
2. Give It Away
3. Californication
4. Scar Tissue
5. Soul To Squeeze
6. Otherside
7. Suck My Kiss
8. By The Way
9. Parallel Universe
10. Breaking The Girl
11. My Friends
12. Higher Ground
13. Universally Speaking
14. Road Trippin'
15. Fortune Faded
16. Save The Population

Live In Hyde Park
Release Year: 2004
Label: Warner Brothers
Producer: Rick Rubin

Track Listing:
Disc One
1. Intro
2. Can't Stop
3. Around The World
4. Scar Tissue
5. By The Way

6. Fortune Faded
7. I Feel Love
8. Otherside
9. Easily
10. Universally Speaking
11. Get On Top
12. Brandy
13. Don't Forget Me
14. Rolling Sly Stone

Disc Two
1. Throw Away Your Television
2. Leverage Of Space
3. Purple Stain
4. The Zephyr Song
5. Mini-Epic
6. Californication
7. Right On Time
8. Parallel Universe
9. Drum Homage Medley
10. Under The Bridge
11. Black Cross
12. Flea's Trumpet Treated by John
13. Give It Away

appendix 2
live dates: 1983-2004

Date	Location	Venue
05.11.83	Tijuana, Mexico	Rancho Grande
07.31.83	Los Angeles CA	Al's Bar
08.04.83	Los Angeles CA	The Plant
04.24.84	San Diego CA	Rodeo
06.16.84	Los Angeles CA	Stardust Ballroom
09.07.84	Los Angeles CA	Fender In'l Ballroom
09.26.84	Los Angeles CA	The Roxy
10.03.84	Sacramento CA	Beaverbrook's North
10.14.84	San Diego CA	Rodeo
12.06.84	Washington DC	Ontario Theater
12.16.84	Oklahoma City OK	The Bowery
12.31.84	Hollywood CA	Club Lingerie
01.06.85	Hollywood CA	Club Lingerie
01.07.85	San Francisco CA	I-Beam
02.05.85	Costa Mesa CA	Deja Vu
04.19.85	Los Angeles CA	Whisky A Go Go
07.18.85	Solana Beach CA	Belly Up Tavern
07.25.85	Los Angeles CA	The Palace
07.26.85	Huntington CA	Spatz
08.17.85	Goarshausen, Germany	Rockpalast Festival
09.13.85	San Diego CA	SDSU
09.14.85	Irvine CA	Irvine Meadows
09.27.85	San Francisco CA	Warfield Theater
09.28.85	Irvine CA	UC Irvine's Crawford Hall
10.13.85	Sacramento CA	Club Can't Tell
10.26.85	Chicago IL	Cabaret Metro
10.31.85	New York NY	The Ritz

11.07.85	Philadelphia PA	Chestnut Cabaret
12.08.85	Oklahoma City OK	Quicksilvers
12.10.85	Dallas TX	Theater Gallery
12.11.85	Houston TX	Rockefeller's
12.12.85	Austin TX	Liberty Lunch
01.16.86	San Francisco CA	Wolfgang's
01.18.86	Santa Cruz CA	The Catalyst
01.25.86	Pomona CA	Pomona Valley Auditorium
02.01.86	Chicago IL	Mandel Hall
02.02.86	Chicago IL	The Vic Theater
02.05.86	Los Angeles CA	The Palace
02.06.86	Solana Beach CA	Belly Up Tavern
02.07.86	Long Beach CA	Fenders Ballroom
02.16.86	San Clemente CA	Coach House
02.24.86	Long Beach CA	Bogarts
03.07.86	San Diego CA	UCSD Gym
03.28.86	Irvine CA	UCI
04.25.86	Morgantown WV	Underground Railroad
05.02.86	Seattle WA	Astor Park
05.03.86	Seattle WA	Astor Park
05.12.86	Los Angeles CA	Olympic Auditorium
05.26.86	Los Angeles CA	The Roxy
06.02.86	Austin TX	Auditorium Shores: Riverfest
06.28.86	Irvine CA	Irvine Meadows
08.28.86	Solana Beach CA	Belly Up Tavern
08.29.86	Hollywood CA	Hollywood Palladium
09.03.86	Atlanta GA	688 Club
10.31.86	Los Angeles CA	UCLA Ackerman Hall
11.21.86	Dallas TX	New Longhorn
11.23.86	Austin TX	The Ritz
11.24.86	Saint Louis MO	Mississippi Nights
11.29.86	Indianapolis IN	Hoosier Ballroom
12.03.86	Toronto, Canada	Lee's Palace

12.10.86	Washington DC	9:30 Club
12.11.86	Washington DC	9:30 Club
01.09.87	Los Angeles CA	Fenders
02.24.87	New York NY	The Ritz
04.06.87	Sacramento CA	Danceteria
04.09.87	San Francisco CA	The Fillmore
06.05.87	San Diego CA	North Park Lions Club
06.14.87	Fullerton CA	Goodies
06.27.87	Seattle WA	Moore Theater
07.10.87	Santa Cruz CA	The Catalyst
08.01.87	Pasadena CA	Perkins Palace
10.24.87	Syracuse NY	The Horizon
10.27.87	Washington DC	9:30 Club
11.08.87	Pittsburgh PA	The Graffiti
11.14.87	Chicago IL	Cabaret Metro
12.04.87	St. Petersburg FL	Jannus Landing
12.11.87	Austin TX	Texas Tavern
12.12.87	San Antonio TX	Woodlawn Theater
12.14.87	Oklahoma City OK	VZD's
12.26.87	Anaheim CA	Celebrity Theater
12.30.87	Vancouver BC	Graceland
01.20.88	Hollywood CA	Palomino Club
01.30.88	Paris FR	Rex Club
02.17.88	Brussels, Belgium	BRT Studios
02.17.88	Brussels	Ancienne Belgique
02.18.88	Eindhoven, Netherlands	De Effenaar
02.19.88	Utrecht, Netherlands	Tivoli
02.20.88	Amsterdam, Netherlands	Paradiso
03.11.88	Northridge CA	Cal State Events Center
03.12.88	Irvine CA	Crawford Hall
03.14.88	San Diego CA	SDSU Montezuma Hall
03.27.88	Los Angeles CA	John Anson Ford Theater
04.02.88	Los Angeles CA	Raji's
04.08.88	Santa Cruz CA	The Catalyst

04.09.88	San Francisco CA	The Filmore
04.14.88	St. Louis MO	Mississippi Nights
04.15.88	Chicago IL	Riviera
04.22.88	New York NY	NYU Auditorium
05.01.88	Washington DC	The Bayou
05.02.88	Berlin, Germany	The Loft
05.11.88	Tijuana, Mexico	Rancho Grande
05.23.88	Landgraaf, Netherlands	Pinkpop Festival
05.29.88	Bielefeld, Germany	PC69
06.04.88	Seinäjoki, Finland	Provinssi Rockfest
09.17.88	Los Angeles CA	John Anson Ford Theater
10.08.88	Los Angeles CA	John Anson Ford Theater
10.09.88	Columbus OH	Octoke Gym
11.16.88	Minneapolis MN	First Avenue Club
11.26.88	Long Beach CA	Cal State Multipurpose Room
11.29.88	Long Beach CA	L.A. Magical Moments
03.09.89	Austin TX	Opera House
03.10.89	San Antonio TX	Showcase Special Events Center
03.11.89	Houston TX	Ensemble Theater
04.07.89	San Francisco CA	The Fillmore
04.28.89	Long Island NY	Sundance Club
06.03.89	Tijuana, Mexico	Iguanas
07.07.89	Hollywood CA	The Palace
09.09.89	Seattle WA	Moore Theater
09.10.89	Portland OR	Starry Night
09.15.89	San Francisco CA	The Fillmore
09.16.89	San Francisco CA	The Fillmore
09.22.89	Hollywood CA	Palladium
09.23.89	Tijuana, Mexico	Iguanas
09.30.89	Houston TX	Ensemble Warehouse
10.04.89	St. Louis MO	Mississippi Nights
10.05.89	St. Louis MO	Mississippi Nights
10.08.89	Minneapolis MN	1st Avenue

10.12.89	Chicago IL	The Vic Theater
10.20.89	Boston MA	Channel
10.24.89	Buffalo NY	BSC Student Union
		Social Hall
10.27.89	New York NY	The Ritz
11.12.89	Brooklyn NY	L'Amours
11.13.89	Poughkeepsie NY	The Chance
11.15.89	Baltimore MD	Studio 10
11.17.89	Washington DC	Lisner Auditorium
11.21.89	Columbus OH	Phantasy Theater
11.22.89	Detroit MI	The Latin Quarter
11.25.89	Chicago IL	Riviera Theater
11.27.89	Madison WI	Barrymore Theater
12.01.89	Atlanta GA	Fox Theater
12.15.89	New Orleans LA	Saenger Performing
		Arts Center
12.16.89	Denver CO	Indoor Sports
		Complex
12.28.89	San Francisco CA	Warfield Theater
12.31.89	Los Angeles CA	Sports Arena
01.26.90	Kawasaki, Japan	Club Citta
02.02.90	Sheffield, UK	Polytechnic
02.03.90	Glasgow, UK	Queen Margaret
	Union	
02.05.90	Edinburgh, UK	Network
02.06.90	Newcastle, UK	Riverside Club
02.07.90	Leeds, UK	Leeds University
02.09.90	Norwich, UK	U.E.A.
02.10.90	Portsmouth, UK	Polytechnic
		Student's Union
02.11.90	London, UK	Astoria
02.13.90	Gent, Belgium	Vooruit
02.14.90	Tilburg, Netherlands	Noorderligt
02.16.90	Utrecht, Netherlands	Tivoli
02.17.90	Amsterdam, Netherlands	Paradiso
02.18.90	Rotterdam, Netherlands	Night Town
02.19.90	Bonn, Germany	Biskuithalle
02.21.90	Hamburg, Germany	Hamburg Docks
02.22.90	Oberhausen, Germany	Musik Circus

02.23.90	Frankfurt, Germany	Batschkapp
02.25.90	Munich, Germany	Nachtwerk
02.26.90	Vienna, Austria	Das Z
02.28.90	Zurich, Switzerland	Rote Fabrik
03.01.90	Lyon, France	Le Truck
03.02.90	Besançon, France	Salle Mont Joye
03.04.90	Paris, France	Elysee Montmartre
03.16.90	Daytona Beach FL	MTV Spring Break
04.26.90	New York NY	Ritz
04.27.90	New York NY	Ritz
05.01.90	Boston MA	Orpheum Theater
05.02.90	Boston MA	Orpheum Theater
05.06.90	Durham NC	University Of North Carolina
05.29.90	Dallas TX	Bronco Bowl
06.01.90	Phoenix AZ	Mesa Amphitheater
06.04.90	Landgraff, Netherlands	Pinkpop Festival
07.21.90	Oakland CA	Henry J. Kaiser Auditorium
12.31.90	San Francisco CA	Civic Auditorium
10.16.91	Madison WI	Oscar Mayer Theater
10.17.91	Dekalb IL	Duke Ellington Ballroom
10.19.91	Ames IA	Stephens Auditorium
10.20.91	Omaha NE	Peony Park Ballroom
10.22.91	Milwaukee WI	Central Park Ballroom
10.23.91	East Lansing MI	M.S.U. Auditorium
10.25.91	Pittsburgh PA	A.J. Palumbo Theater
10.26.91	Cleveland OH	Music Hall
10.27.91	Rochester NY	Auditorium Theater
10.29.91	Toronto, Canada	Toronto Concert Hall
10.30.91	Toronto, Canada	Toronto Concert Hall

11.01.91	Boston MA	Walter Brown Arena
11.02.91	Burlington VT	Memorial Auditorium
11.03.91	Springfield MA	Civic Center
11.05.91	Troy NY	RPI Fieldhouse
11.07.91	Syracuse NY	Landmark Theater
11.08.91	Upper Darby PA	Tower Theater
11.09.91	Washington DC	Render Arena
11.11.91	New York NY	Roseland Ballroom
11.12.91	New York NY	Roseland Ballroom
11.13.91	Warwick RI	Rocky Point Palladium
11.15.91	New York NY	Roseland Ballroom
11.16.91	New York NY	Roseland Ballroom
11.17.91	State College PA	Rec. Hall PSU
11.19.91	Columbus OH	Veterans Memorial
11.20.91	Kalamazoo MI	Wings Stadium
11.22.91	Detroit MI	State Theater
11.23.91	Detroit MI	State Theater
11.24.91	Indianapolis IN	Convention Center
11.26.91	Normal IL ISU	Braden Auditorium
11.27.91	Cincinnatti OH	Gardens
11.29.91	Chicago IL	Veterans Memorial
11.30.91	St. Paul MN	Roy Wilkins Auditorium
12.02.91	St. Louis MO	American Theater
12.03.91	St. Louis MO	American Theater
12.04.91	Kansas City KS	Memorial Hall
12.06.91	New Orleans LA	State Palace Theater
12.07.91	Houston TX	Unicorn Ballroom
12.08.91	Houston TX	Vatican
12.10.91	Austin TX	City Coliseum
12.11.91	Dallas TX	Bronco Bowl
12.14.91	Denver CO	Denver Coliseum
12.27.91	Los Angeles CA	Sports Arena
12.28.91	San Diego CA	Del Mar Pavilion
12.29.91	Tempe AZ	ASU Center

12.31.91	San Francisco CA	MTV Studios
12.31.91	San Francisco CA	Cow Palace
01.03.92	Seattle WA	Arena
02.02.92	Hamburg, Germany	Hamburg Docks
02.03.92	Vancouver BC	P.N.E Forum
02.11.92	Rotterdam, Netherlands	The Ahoy
02.13.92	Hamburg, Germany	Hamburg Docks
02.15.92	Deinze, Belgium	Brielport
02.16.92	Paris, France	Le Zéénith
02.22.92	New York NY	SNL Studios
02.25.92	Munich, Germany	Theaterfabrik
02.26.92	Munich, Germany	Theaterfabrik
02.27.92	Frankfurt, Germany	Kongresshalle
03.01.92	Milan, Italy	Palatrussardi
03.07.92	Dublin, Ireland	The Point
03.10.92	Glasgow, UK	Barrowland Ballroom
03.13.92	London, UK	Brixton Academy
03.16.92	Bielefeld, Germany	PC 69
03.18.92	Ludwigsburg, Germany	Forum Am Schlosspark
03.19.92	Düsseldorf, Germany	Phillipshalle
03.20.92	Neumarkt, Germany	Jurahalle
03.22.92	Berlin, Germany	Die Halle
04.04.92	Los Angeles CA	The Palladium
05.14.92	Brisbane, Australia	Festival Hall
05.15.92	Sydney, Australia	Hordern Pavilion
05.16.92	Sydney, Australia	Hordern Pavilion
05.19.92	Adelaide, Australia	Barton Theater
05.20.92	Melbourne, Australia	Festival Hall
05.23.92	Auckland, New Zealand	Super Top
05.24.92	Wellington, N.Z.	Town Hall
05.25.92	Auckland, New Zealand	Super Top
07.05.92	Werchter, Belgium	Werchter Festival
07.18.92	San Francisco CA Amphitheater	Shoreline
07.19.92	San Francisco CA Amphitheater	Shoreline
07.21.92	Vancouver, Canada	UBC Field

07.22.92	Bremerton WA	Kitsap County Fairgrounds
07.25.92	Denver CO	Fiddler's Green
07.27.92	St. Louis MO	Riverport Amphitheater
07.28.92	Cincinnati OH	Riverbend
07.29.92	Cleveland OH	Blossom Music Center
07.31.92	Detroit MI	Pine Knob
08.01.92	Detroit MI	Pine Knob
08.02.92	Chicago IL	World Amphitheater
08.04.92	Saratoga Springs NY	Performing Arts Ctr
08.05.92	Toronto CA	Molson Park
08.07.92	Boston MA	Great Woods
08.08.92	Boston MA	Great Woods
08.09.92	Long Island NY	Jones Beach
08.11.92	Long Island NY	Jones Beach
08.12.92	Stanhope NJ	Waterloo Village
08.14.92	Alexandria VA	Lake Fairfax
08.16.92	Pittsburgh PA	Starlake Amphitheater
08.18.92	Raleigh NC	Walnut Creek Amphitheater
08.20.92	Atlanta GA	Lakewood Amphitheater
08.22.92	Miami FL	Bicentennial Park
08.23.92	Orlando FL	Central Fairgrounds
08.25.92	Charlotte NC	Blockbuster Pavilion
08.28.92	Minneapolis MN	Harriet Island
08.29.92	Troy WI	Alpine Valley
09.01.92	Atlanta GA	Lakewood Amphitheater
09.04.92	New Orleans LA	UNO Soccer Field
09.05.92	Houston TX	Ft. Bend Cty. Fairgrounds
09.06.92	Dallas TX	Starplex Amphitheater
09.08.92	Phoenix AZ	Desert Sky Pavilion

09.11.92	Los Angeles CA	Irvine Meadows
09.12.92	Los Angeles CA	Irvine Meadows
09.13.92	Los Angeles CA	Irvine Meadows
09.27.92	Los Angeles CA	Hollywood Palladium
10.06.92	Brisbane, Australia	Entertainment Center
10.07.92	Brisbane, Australia	Entertainment Center
10.09.92	Sydney, Australia	Entertainment Center
10.10.92	Sydney, Australia	Entertainment Center
10.13.92	Sydney, Australia	Entertainment Center
10.15.92	Adelaide, Australia Showgrounds	Adelaide
10.17.92	Perth, Australia	Entertainment Center
10.20.92	Melbourne, Australia	Entertainment Center
10.21.92	Melbourne, Australia	Flinders Park Tennis Center
10.27.92	Wellington, N. Z.	Winter Show Buildings
10.28.92	Auckland, New Zealand	Mt. Smart Supertop
12.12.92	New York NY	*The Ben Stiller Show*
01.15.93	Sao Paulo, Brazil Festival	Hollywood Rock
01.22.93	Rio de Janeiro, Brazil Festival	Hollywood Rock
02.19.93	New Orleans LA	The Quad
02.24.93	Los Angeles CA	Shrine Auditorium
12.31.93	Seattle WA	MTV's *Live and Loud*
08.10.94	Los Angeles CA	Club Lingerie
08.14.94	Saugerties NY	Woodstock II Festival
08.17.94	New York NY	Academy Theater

08.19.94	New York NY	Roseland Ballroom
08.25.94	Dublin, Ireland	Dalymont Park
08.27.94	Hasselt, Belgium	Pukkelpop Festival
08.28.94	Reading, UK	Reading Festival
08.31.94	Madrid, Spain	Las Ventas Bullring
09.03.94	Roskilde, Denmark	Heyday Festival
09.04.94	Köln, Germany	Sportshalle
10.19.94	Pasadena CA	Rose Bowl
10.21.94	Pasadena CA	Rose Bowl
09.07.95	New York NY	MTV Awards
09.27.95	London, UK	Subterrania Club
09.29.95	Dublin, Ireland	The Point
09.30.95	Dublin, Ireland	The Point
10.01.95	Dublin, Ireland	The Point
10.03.95	London, UK	Brixton Academy
10.04.95	London, UK	Brixton Academy
10.06.95	Manchester, UK	Apollo
10.08.95	Brussels, Belgium	Forest National
10.09.95	Hamburg, Germany	Sportshalle
10.11.95	Berlin, Germany	Deutschlandhalle
10.12.95	Köln, Germany	Sportshalle
10.14.95	Stockholm, Sweden	The Globe
10.16.95	Rotterdam, Netherlands	The Ahoy
10.18.95	Paris, France	Le Zenith
10.20.95	Zurich, Switzerland	Hallenstadion
10.21.95	Milan, Italy	Forum Arena
10.23.95	Barcelona, Spain	Palau D'esports
02.06.96	Philadelphia PA	The Spectrum
02.08.96	Boston MA	Fleet Center
02.09.96	New York NY Garden	Madison Square
02.11.96	Albany NY	Knickerbocker Arena
02.12.96	Worcester MA	Centrum
02.13.96	New York NY	*David Letterman Show*
02.14.96	Landover MD	U.S. Air Arena
02.16.96	Nassau NY	Nassau Coliseum
03.06.96	Chicago IL	United Center

03.07.96	Auburn Hills MI	The Palace
03.11.96	Indianapolis IN	Market Square Arena
03.12.96	Cleveland OH	Gund Arena
03.14.96	Pittsburgh PA	Civic Arena
03.16.96	Kansas City MO	Municipal Auditorium
03.18.96	St. Louis MO	Kiel Center
04.01.96	Denver CO	McNichols Arena
04.03.96	Phoenix AZ	America West Arena
04.04.96	Los Angeles CA	The Great Western Forum
04.06.96	San Francisco CA	Cow Palace
04.08.96	Sacramento CA	Arco Arena
04.10.96	Portland OR	The Rose Garden
04.12.96	Seattle WA	The Key Arena
04.13.96	Vancouver, Canada	Pacific Coliseum
04.16.96	San Diego CA	Sports Arena
05.03.96	Auckland, New Zealand	Supertop
05.04.96	Wellington, N.Z.	Queens Wharf
05.06.96	Melbourne, Australia	Flinders Park
05.07.96	Melbourne, Australia	Flinders Park
05.10.96	Perth, Australia	Entertainment Center
05.12.96	Adelaide, Australia	Entertainment Center
05.14.96	Sydney, Australia	Entertainment Center
05.15.96	Sydney, Australia	Entertainment Center
05.17.96	Brisbane, Australia	Entertainment Center
06.15.96	Irvine CA	Irvine Meadows
06.16.96	San Francisco CA	Golden Gate Park
06.25.96	Budapest, Hungary	Kissstadion
06.26.96	Prague, Czechoslovakia	Sports Hall
06.28.96	St. Gallen, Switzerland	St. Gallen Festival
06.29.96	Roskilde, Denmark	Roskilde Festival
06.30.96	Turku, Finland	Ruisrock Festival

07.03.96	Oslo, Norway	Spektrum
07.05.96	Belfort, France	Eurockeennes
07.06.96	Torhout, Belgium	Torhout Festival
07.07.96	Werchter, Belgium	Werchter Festival
07.09.96	Paris, France	Bercy
07.11.96	London, UK	Wembley
01.24.97	New York NY	*David Letterman Show*
07.26.97	Yamanasi, Japan	Fuji Rock Festival
06.05.98	Silver Lake CA	KBLT Radio
06.13.98	Washington DC	RFK Stadium
06.28.98	Hollywood CA	Moguls
09.05.98	Las Vegas NV	Huntridge Theater
09.06.98	Las Vegas NV	Huntridge Theater
09.18.98	Chico CA	Field Of Dreams
09.19.98	Reno NV	Livestock Arena
09.20.98	Stockton CA	Civic Auditorium
05.15.99	Portland OR	Roseland Theater
05.16.99	Seattle WA	Moore Theater
05.20.99	Minneapolis MN	Coliseum
05.22.99	Chicago IL Theater	New World Music
05.23.99	St. Louis MO Amphitheater	Riverport
05.25.99	Pontiac MI	Clutch Cargo
05.27.99	Philadelphia PA	Theater of the Living Arts
05.29.99	Baltimore MD	PSInet Stadium
05.30.99	Mansfield MA	Tweeter Center
06.02.99	Hamburg, Germany	Kulturfabrik Kampnagel
06.04.99	Stockholm, Sweden	Sodra Teatern
06.08.99	Paris, France	Elysée Montmartre
06.09.99	Paris, France	Canal+ Studio
06.11.99	London, UK	Camden Palace
06.14.99	Milan, Italy	MTV Studios
06.18.99	Mountain View CA Amphitheater	Shoreline

06.19.99	Irvine CA	Irvine Meadows
06.25.99	Hollywood CA	Palladium
07.22.99	Toronto, Canada	Yonge Street
07.25.99	Rome NY	Woodstock Festival
08.10.99	Toronto, Canada	Edge 102 / The Blue Line
08.14.99	Moscow, Russia	Red Square
08.18.99	Wiesen, Austria	Wiesen Festival
08.20.99	Köln, Germany	Bizarre Festival
08.21.99	Copenhagen, Denmark	Club Denmark Hallen
08.22.99	Stockholm, Sweden	99 Festival
08.25.99	Nîmes, France	Arêne de Nîmes
08.26.99	Paris, France	Le Zéenith
08.27.99	Hasselt, Belgium	Pukkelpop Festival
08.29.99	Reading, UK	Reading Festival
08.30.99	Leeds, UK	Temple Newsam Park
09.04.99	Verona, Italy	Festival Bar TV
09.23.99	Toronto, Canada	Much Music Video Awards
10.02.99	Santiago, Chile	Estacion Mapocho
10.03.99	Santiago, Chile	Estacion Mapocho
10.05.99	Buenos Aires, Argentina	Luna Park
10.06.99	Buenos Aires, Argentina	Luna Park
10.08.99	Sao Paulo, Brazil	Credicard Hall
10.11.99	Mexico City, Mexico	Sports Palace
10.26.99	New York NY	World Trade Center
10.29.99	Helsinki, Finland	Hartwall Arena
10.30.99	Helsinki, Finland	Hartwall Arena
11.01.99	Oslo, Norway	Spektrum
11.03.99	Götenborg, Sweden	Scandinavium
11.04.99	Hamburg, Germany	Sportshalle
11.06.99	London, UK	Wembley Arena
11.08.99	Berlin, Germany	The Arena
11.10.99	Den Haag, Netherlands	Statenhal
11.11.99	Böblingen, Germany	Sportshalle
11.13.99	Zurich, Switzerland	Hallen Stadium
11.14.99	Milan, Italy	Forum
11.16.99	Paris, France	Bercy

11.18.99	Bordeaux, France	Patinoire
11.19.99	Barcelona, Spain Hebron	Pabellon Valle de
11.21.99	Madrid, Spain	La Cubierta Bullring
11.22.99	Lisbon, Portugal	Pavilhao Atlantico
12.08.99	Las Vegas NV	*Billboard* Music Awards
12.26.99	San Diego CA	Cox Arena
12.28.99	San Francisco CA	Cow Palace
12.29.99	Sacramento CA	Arco Arena
12.31.99	Los Angeles CA	Great Western Forum
01.08.00	Tokyo, Japan	Budokan
01.09.00	Tokyo, Japan	Budokan
01.10.00	Tokyo, Japan	Budokan
01.13.00	Yokohama, Japan	Pacifico
01.14.00	Osaka, Japan	Castle Hall
01.23.00	Gold Coast, Australia	Gold Coast Parkland
01.24.00	Brisbane, Australia	Entertainment Center
01.26.00	Sydney, Australia	RAS Showgrounds
01.27.00	Sydney, Australia	Entertainment Center
01.28.00	Sydney, Australia	Entertainment Center
01.30.00	Melbourne, Australia	Showgrounds
02.01.00	Melbourne, Australia	Entertainment Center
02.02.00	Melbourne, Australia	Entertainment Center
02.04.00	Adelaide, Australia	Showgrounds
02.06.00	Perth, Australia	Bassendean Oval
02.07.00	Perth, Australia	Entertainment Center
03.24.00	Minneapolis MN	Target Center
03.25.00	Madison WI	Dane County Exp. Ctr

03.27.00	Carbondale IL	SIU Arena
03.28.00	Champaign IL	Assembly Arena
03.30.00	Dayton OH	Nutter Center
03.31.00	Columbus OH	Value City Arena
04.02.00	Amherst MA	Mullins Center
04.03.00	Albany NY	Pepsi Center
04.05.00	Penn State U. PA	Bryce Jordan Arena
04.06.00	Roanoke VA	Civic Center
04.08.00	Bloomington IN	Assembly Hall
04.09.00	Lexington KY	Rupp Arena
04.11.00	Knoxville TN	Thompson Bolling Arena
04.12.00	Chattanooga TN	UTC Arena
04.25.00	Omaha NE	Civic Auditorium
04.26.00	Iowa City IA	Carver Hawkeye
04.28.00	Columbia MO	Hearnes Center
04.29.00	Oklahoma City OK	Myriad Center
05.01.00	Little Rock AR	Barton Arena
05.02.00	Austin TX	Frank Erwin Center
05.04.00	New Orleans LA	Lakefront Arena
05.05.00	Pensacola FL	Civic Center
05.07.00	Greenville SC	Bi-Lo Center
05.08.00	Norfolk VA	Scope Arena
05.10.00	Baltimore MD	Baltimore Arena
05.11.00	WilkesBarre PA	NEPA Arena
05.13.00	Providence RI	Civic Center
05.14.00	Portland ME	Cumberland Civic Center
05.27.00	George WA	The Gorge
05.28.00	Vancouver BC	GM Place
05.31.00	Salt Lake City UT	E Center
06.02.00	Phoenix AZ	Desert Sky Amphitheater
06.03.00	Albuquerque NM	Pitt Arena
06.05.00	Houston TX	Compaq Center
06.06.00	Dallas TX	Starplex Amphitheater
06.08.00	Atlanta GA	Lakewood Amphitheater
06.09.00	Charlotte NC	Blockbuster Pavilion

06.11.00	Raleigh NC	Alltell Amphitheater
06.12.00	Nashville TN Amphitheater	Starwood
06.14.00	Palm Beach FL	Mars Music Amphitheater
06.15.00	Orlando FL	Orlando Arena
06.23.00	Seattle WA	Memorial Stadium
06.28.00	Bonner Springs KS	Sandstone Amphitheater
06.29.00	St. Louis MO Amphitheater	Riverport
07.01.00	Moline IL Quad	The Mark of the
07.02.00	Milwaukee WI	Summerfest
07.04.00	Louisville KY	Freedom Hall
07.05.00	Grand Rapids MI	Van Andreal Arena
07.07.00	Indianapolis IN	Deer Creek Ampitheatre
07.08.00	Cleveland OH	Blossom Music Center
07.10.00	Bristow VA	Nissan Pavilion
07.11.00	Camden NJ	E Center
07.13.00	Hartford CT	The Meadows
07.14.00	Holmdel NJ	PNC Arts Center
07.15.00	Mansfield MA	Tweeter Center
07.17.00	Hershey PA	Hershey Stadium
07.26.00	Boston MA	Tweeter Center
07.30.00	Saratoga NY	SPAC
07.31.00	Holmdel NJ	PNC Arts Center
08.02.00	Tinley Park IL Theater	New World Music
08.03.00	Cincinnati OH	Riverbend Amphitheater
08.05.00	Latrobe PA	Rolling Rock Festival
08.07.00	Detroit MI	Pine Knob
08.08.00	Detroit MI	Pine Knob
08.10.00	Charleston WV	Civic Center
08.12.00	Wantaugh NY	Jones Beach

08.13.00	Wantaugh NY	Jones Beach
08.15.00	Buffalo NY	Darien Lake
08.16.00	Toronto CA	Molson Amphitheater
08.18.00	Quebec CA	Colisée Pepsi
08.19.00	Montreal CA	Molson Center
09.01.00	Irvine CA	Irvine Meadows
09.02.00	Irvine CA	Irvine Meadows
09.04.00	Chula Vista CA	Coors Amphitheater
09.07.00	New York NY	Radio City Music Hall
09.09.00	Mountain View CA Amphitheater	Shoreline
09.10.00	Sacramento CA	Valley Amphitheater
09.12.00	Fresno CA	Selland Arena
09.13.00	Las Vegas NV	Thomas and Mack Center
09.15.00	Casper NV	Casper Events Center
09.16.00	Denver CO	Fiddlers Green
09.18.00	Boise ID	Boise Center
09.19.00	Spokane WA	Spokane Arena
09.21.00	Portland OR	Memorial Coliseum
09.22.00	Seattle WA	Memorial Coliseum
10.28.00	Mountain View CA Amphitheater	Shoreline
10.29.00	Mountain View CA Amphitheater	Shoreline
11.05.00	Seattle WA	Key Arena
11.06.00	Seattle WA	Key Arena
11.30.00	Los Angeles CA	Shrine Auditorium
01.21.01	Rio De Janeiro, Brazil	Rock In Rio III Festival
01.24.01	Buenos Aires, Argentina	Estadio Velez Sarsfield
03.01.01	Hollywood CA	Hollywood Palladium
03.14.01	New York NY	Irving Plaza

08.01.01	New York NY	Hammerstein Ballroom
08.18.01	Stafford, UK	Weston Park
08.19.01	Chelmsford, UK	Hylands Park
08.21.01	Parken, Denmark	Parken Stadion
08.23.01	Utrecht, Netherlands	Prins Van Oranjchal
08.25.01	Dublin, Ireland	Slane Castle
12.14.01	Silver Lake CA	Paramour Estate
04.13.02	Los Angeles CA	Universal Amphitheater
05.04.02	Paris, France	Special "Secret" Show
05.17.02	Los Angeles CA	Vans Skate Park
05.26.02	Naples, Italy	Festival Bar TV
05.31.02	London, UK	BBC Studios
06.04.02	Paris, France	Olympia
06.07.02	Hamburg, Germany	Saturn
06.10.02	Madrid, Spain	Circulo de Bellas Artes
06.15.02	Imola, Italy	Heineken Jammin' Fest
06.17.02	Barcelona, Spain	Olimpic De Badalone
06.19.02	Nice, France	Palais Nikaia
06.20.02	Lyon, France	Halle Tony Garnier
06.22.02	Neuhausen, Germany	Southside Festival
06.23.02	Scheesel, Germany	Hurricane Festival
06.25.02	Dublin, Ireland	Lansdowne Road
06.26.02	London, UK	London Arena
06.28.02	Roskilde, Denmark	Roskilde Festival
06.29.02	Werchter, Belgium	Werchter Festival
07.09.02	New York NY	Ellis Island
07.10.02	Atlanta GA	Dekalb Civic Center
07.26.02	Seoul, Korea	Chamsil Sports Complex
07.28.02	Niigata, Japan	Fuji Rock Festival
07.31.02	Honolulu HI	Neal S. Blaisdell Center

08.03.02	Las Vegas NV	Backyard BBQ
08.07.02	Toronto, Canada	The Edge 102.1
09.27.02	Guadalajara, Mexico	Plaza de Toros
09.29.02	Mexico City, Mexico	Foro Sol
10.02.02	San Jose, Costa Rica Stadium	Rosabal Cordero
10.04.02	Panama City, Panama Center	Atlapa Convention
10.06.02	Caracus, Venezuela	Valle del Pop
10.09.02	Santiago, Chile	Pista Athletica
10.11.02	Rio de Janeiro, Brazil	ATL Hall
10.12.02	São Paulo, Bazil	Pacaembu Stadium
10.14.02	Porto Allegre, Brazil	Ginasio do Gigantinho
10.16.02	Buenos Aires, Argentina	River Plate Stadium
10.26.02	Los Angeles CA	Wiltern Theater
11.02.02	Chiba City, Japan	Makuhari Messe
11.03.02	Chiba City, Japan	Makuhari Messe
11.05.02	Osaka, Japan	Osaka-Jo Hall
11.06.02	Osaka, Japan	Osaka-Jo Hall
11.10.02	Saitama, Japan	Super Arena
11.12.02	Fukuoka, Japan	Marine Messe
11.13.02	Nagoya, Japan	Rainbow Hall
11.22.02	Christchurch, N.Z.	QE2 Stadium
11.24.02	Auckland, New Zealand	Western Springs
11.26.02	Brisbane, Australia	Entertainment Center
11.29.02	Sydney, Australia	Aussie Stadium
12.01.02	Melbourne, Australia	Telstra Dome
12.03.02	Adelaide, Australia	Entertainment Center
12.06.02	Perth, Australia	Perth Dome
12.08.02	Singapore	Indoor Arena
12.10.02	Bangkok, Thailand	Impact Arena
12.30.02	Las Vegas NV	Hard Rock Hotel
12.31.02	Las Vegas NV	Hard Rock Hotel
01.24.03	Lisbon, Portugal	Atlantic Pavilion
01.25.03	Lisbon, Portugal	Atlantic Pavilion
01.27.03	Madrid, Spain	Palacio Vistalegre

01.28.03	Madrid, Spain	Palacio Vistalegre
01.30.03	Milan, Italy	Filaforum
01.31.03	Milan, Italy	Filaforum
02.02.03	Rome, Italy	Palaeur
02.03.03	Rome, Italy	Palaeur
02.05.03	Bologna, Italy	Palamalaguti
02.07.03	Dortmund, Germany	Westfalenhalle
02.09.03	Dresden, Germany	Messehalle
02.10.03	Berlin, Germany	Velodrome
02.12.03	Paris, France	Bercy
02.13.03	Paris, France	Bercy
03.05.03	Glasgow, UK	SECC
03.06.03	Glasgow, UK	SECC
03.08.03	London, UK	Docklands Arena
03.09.03	London, UK	Docklands Arena
03.11.03	Manchester, UK	Evening News Arena
03.12.03	Manchester, UK	Evening News Arena
03.14.03	Antwerp, Belgium	Sportpaleis
03.16.03	Zurich, Switzerland	Hallenstadion
03.17.03	Munich, Germany	Olympiahalle
03.19.03	Rotterdam, Netherlands	The Ahoy
03.20.03	Rotterdam, Netherlands	The Ahoy
03.22.03	Hamburg, Germany	Colour Line Arena
03.24.03	Helsinki, Finland	Hartwall Arena
03.25.03	Turku, Finland	Turku Hall
03.27.03	Oslo, Norway	Spectrum
03.29.03	Stockholm, Sweden	Globe
04.27.03	Indio CA	Empire Polo Field
05.01.03	St. Paul MN	Xcel Energy Center
05.02.03	Madison WI	Alliant Energy Center
05.04.03	Omaha NE	Omaha Civic Auditorium
05.05.03	Kansas City MO	Kemper Arena
05.07.03	St. Louis MO	Savvis Center
05.09.03	Moline IL	Mark Of The Quad Cities
05.10.03	Grand Rapids MI	Van Andel Arena

05.12.03	Ottawa, Canada	Corel Center
05.13.03	Toronto, Canada	Air Canada Center
05.15.03	Montreal, Canada	Bell Center
05.17.03	Albany NY	Pepsi Arena
05.19.03	East Rutherford NJ	Continental Airlines Arena
05.20.03	New York NY	Madison Square Garden
06.02.03	West Palm Beach FL	Coral Sky Amphitheater
06.03.03	Orlando FL	TD Waterhouse Center
06.05.03	Raleigh NC	Alltel Pavilion
06.06.03	Charlotte NC	Verizon Wireless Amphitheater
06.08.03	Atlanta GA	HiFi Buys Amphitheater
06.10.03	Bossier City LA	CenturyTel Center
06.11.03	New Orleans LA	New Orleans Arena
06.13.03	San Antonio TX	Verizon Wireless Amphitheater
06.14.03	Woodlands TX	C.W. Mitchell Pavilion
06.16.03	Dallas TX	Smirnoff Music Center
06.18.03	Oklahoma City OK	The Ford Center
06.20.03	Englewood CO	Fiddler's Green Amphitheater
06.21.03	Albuquerque NM	Journal Pavilion
08.13.03	Stuttgart, Germany	Schleyerhalle
08.16.03	Staffordshire, UK	Weston Park
08.17.03	Chelmsford, UK	Hylands Park
08.19.03	Berlin, Germany	Wuhlheide
08.21.03	Duisburg, Germany Nord	Landschaftspark
08.23.03	County Meath, Ireland	Slane Castle
08.24.03	Glasgow, UK	Glasgow Green
09.06.03	Bristow VA	Nissan Pavilion
09.07.03	Holmdel NJ	PNC Arts Center
09.09.03	Amherst MA	Mullins Center

09.10.03	Boston MA	Tweeter Center
09.12.03	Philadelphia PA	Tweeter Center
09.13.03	New York NY	Jones Beach
09.16.03	Penn State U. PA	Bryce Jordan Center
09.18.03	Detroit MI Hills	Palace of Auburn
09.19.03	Tinley Park IL	Tweeter Center
09.21.03	Cleveland OH	Gund Arena
09.22.03	Pittsburgh PA	Mellon Arena
09.24.03	E Lansing MI	Breslin Arena
09.25.03	Milwaukee WI	Bradley Center
10.08.03	Las Vegas NV	Mandalay Bay Events Center
10.09.03	Phoenix AZ	Cricket Pavilion
10.11.03	Inglewood CA	Great Western Forum
10.12.03	Irvine CA Amphitheater	Verizon Wireless
10.17.03	Oakland CA	Oakland Coliseum
10.18.03	Sacramento CA	Arco Arena
10.20.03	Portland OR	Memorial Coliseum
10.21.03	Seattle WA	Key Arena
10.23.03	Vancouver, Canada	Pacific Coliseum
10.26.03	Edmonton, Canada	Skyreach
10.27.03	Calgary, Canada	Saddledome
11.15.03	Los Angeles CA	Hollywood Palladium
06.06.04	Eifel/Nürburg, Germany	Rock Am Ring Festival
06.08.04	Milan, Italy	San Siro Stadium
06.10.04	Nr Vienna, Austria	Aerodrome
06.12.04	Dublin, Ireland	Phoenix Park
06.13.04	Edinburgh, UK	Murrayfield
06.15.04	Paris, France	Parc des Princes
06.16.04	Amsterdam, Netherlands	Amsterdam Arena
06.18.04	Manchester, UK	Manchester Stadium
06.19.04	London, UK	Hyde Park
06.20.04	London, UK	Hyde Park

06.23.04	Cardiff, UK	Millennium Stadium
06.25.04	London, UK	Hyde Park
06.27.04	Santiago, Spain	Monte del Gozo
	Auditorium	
07.24.04	Osaka, Japan	Osaka Dome
07.25.04	Yokohama Cty, Japan	International Stadium
10.23.04	Mountain View CA	Bridge School Benefit
10.24.04	Mountain View CA	Bridge School Benefit

index